Rethinking Infrastructure in Latin America and the Caribbean

DIRECTIONS IN DEVELOPMENT
Infrastructure

Rethinking Infrastructure in Latin America and the Caribbean

Spending Better to Achieve More

Marianne Fay, Luis Alberto Andrés, Charles Fox, Ulf Narloch, Stéphane Straub, and Michael Slawson

WORLD BANK GROUP

Contents

Boxes

Figures

Rethinking Infrastructure in Latin America and the Caribbean
http://dx.doi.org/10.1596/978-1-4648-1101-2

Maps

Tables

Rethinking Infrastructure in Latin America and the Caribbean
http://dx.doi.org/10.1596/978-1-4648-1101-2

Acknowledgments

This report is a joint product of the Latin America and Caribbean Region's Vice-Presidency and the Chief Economist Office of the Sustainable Development Practice Group. The task team leaders are Marianne Fay and Luis Alberto Andrés. Contributors include Charles Fox, Ulf Narloch, Michael Slawson, and Stéphane Straub.

The following World Bank colleagues and consultants contributed background papers and substantive inputs: Daniel Benitez, Diana Cubas, Steven Farji, Xijie Lu, Maria Claudia Pachon, and Tatiana Peralta Quiros (Transport); Gabriela Elizondo Azuela, Jiemei Liu, Farah Mohammadzadeh, and Patricia Vargas (Energy and Extractives); Aroha Bahuguna, Christian Borja-Vega, Gustavo Perochena Meza, Diego Rodriguez, Gustavo Saltiel, and Virginia Ziulu (Water); Shohei Nakamura and Carlos Rodriguez Castelan (Poverty); Kevin McCall and Juan Jose Miranda Montero (Environment); Beatriz Eraso, Catalina Marulanda, Emanuela Monteiro, and Carlos Perez-Brito (Social, Urban, Rural, and Resilience); Catiana Garcia-Kilroy, Cledan Mandri-Perrot, Fernanda Ruiz Nunez, and Heinz Rudolph (PPP); Jorge Araujo and Naotaka Sugawara (Fiscal); Sebastian Lopez Azumendi (Institutions); Diego Dorado, Ian Hawkesworth, and Jens Kromann Kristensen (Public Spending Efficiency); Cesar Chaparro Yedro, Tania Ghossein, Khasankhon Khamudkhanov, Federica Saliola, and Mikel Tejada Ibanez (Procurement).

Additional background papers were commissioned from KTH Royal Institute of Technology (Oliver Broad, Mark Howells, and Gustavo de Moura), Fernando Miralles-Wilhelm, and Daniel Nolasco.

The team is grateful for guidance provided by Jorge Familiar Calderon, Vice President of the Latin America and Caribbean Region, and Karin Erika Kemper, Senior Regional Adviser, as well as comments and helpful suggestions from Cecilia Briceño-Garmendia, James Brumby, Uwe Deichman, Alfonso Garcia Mora, Ejaz Ghani, Jesko Hentschel, Jens Kromann Kristensen, Antonio Nucifora, Carlos Perez-Brito, Pablo Saavedra, Jordan Schwartz, Luis Serven, Carlos Silva-Jauregui, Marijn Verhoeven, and Jan Weetjens. Paul Holtz edited the report.

The findings, interpretations, and conclusions expressed in this document are those of the authors and do not necessarily reflect the views of the Executive Directors of the World Bank, the governments they represent, or the counterparts consulted or engaged with during the informal study process. Any factual errors are the responsibility of the team.

About the Authors

Marianne Fay is Chief Economist of the Sustainable Development Vice-Presidency at the World Bank. She previously served as the Chief Economist for Climate Change. She contributed to several World Development Reports, notably the *World Development Report 2010* on Development and Climate Change, which she co-directed, and led a number of recent World Bank reports, such as Inclusive *Green Growth: The Pathway to Sustainable Development* and *Decarbonizing Development: Three Steps to a Zero-Carbon Future*. She has held positions in the Eastern Europe and Central Asia, Latin America and the Caribbean, and Africa regions of the World Bank, working on infrastructure, urbanization, and climate change. She is the author of a number of articles and books on these topics.

Luis Alberto Andrés is Lead Economist in the Water Global Practice at the World Bank. He has held positions in the Sustainable Development Department for the Latin America and the Caribbean and the South Asia regions. He focuses on infrastructure, mainly the water and energy sectors, impact evaluations, private sector participation, regulation, and empirical microeconomics. Before joining the World Bank, he was the Chief of Staff for the Secretary of Fiscal and Social Equity for the government of Argentina and held other positions in the Chief of Cabinet of Ministries and the Ministry of Economy. He holds a PhD in economics from the University of Chicago and has written books, monographs, and articles on development policy issues.

Charles Fox is an analyst based in Washington, DC. He has been heavily involved with the World Bank's Geospatial Operations Support Team (GOST) since its inception. He focuses on applying geospatial analytics and data visualizations to operational problems. Prior to joining the World Bank in 2016, Charles was an analyst with Lazard & Co. Services Ltd., specializing in transactions in the Natural Resources sector and then leveraged transactions with a financial sponsor component. Before Lazard, he worked for Triple Point Investment Management. He holds a BA in economics and management from Oxford University (1st Class).

Ulf Narloch is an economist in the World Bank Group's Climate Change Chief Economist's Office, based in Washington, DC. He works on green growth and climate policies, poverty impacts of climate change, and sustainability measurement and diagnostics. Prior to joining the World Bank in 2013, he was with the United Nations Environment Programme—World Conservation Monitoring Centre (UNEP-WCMC), Bioversity International, the Food and Agriculture Organization (FAO), and the Kiel Institute for the World Economy (IfW). His work focused on the evaluation of economic instruments and household decisions related to land use, farm management, and livelihood strategies. He holds a PhD in land economy from Cambridge University.

Stéphane Straub is a professor of economics at the Toulouse School of Economics, where he has been the head of the development group for many years. He is on sabbatical at the World Bank in Washington, DC, working with the Sustainable Development Practice Group and the Research Department. He works on issues of infrastructure, procurement, and more generally, institutional development in the context of developing countries, on which he has published extensively. He has held academic positions in the United States, the United Kingdom, and France and has been a consultant for several international institutions such as the World Bank, the Inter-American Development Bank, the European Union, and the Asian Development Bank among others. He previously lived for 10 years in Paraguay, where he worked as an entrepreneur, private consultant, government adviser, and university professor.

Michael Slawson's portfolio of work includes helping clients analyze, structure, and finance infrastructure projects. He provides cross-sector technical and analytical consulting for government and donor bank clients, focusing on public-private partnerships, strategic planning, and project finance. Previously, he was an entrepreneur creating a sustainable charcoal production business in an emerging market. He also has worked for Castalia Strategic Advisors, an infrastructure advisory firm. He holds an MA in international economics and international relations from the Johns Hopkins School of Advanced International Studies.

Abbreviations

BPP	Benchmarking Public Procurement
BRT	bus rapid transit
CNG	compressed natural gas
COP21	Paris Climate Conference
DALY	disability-adjusted life years
DFI	development finance institutions
DMU	decision making under uncertainty
EAP	East Asia and the Pacific
ECA	Europe and Central Asia
GEA	Global Energy Assessment
GtO$_2$e	gigatons of carbon dioxide emissions
IA	Infrastructure Australia
IBNET	International Benchmarking Network for Water and Sanitation Utilities
LAC	Latin America and the Caribbean
LPI	Logistics Performance Index
MCC	Mexico, Central America, and the Caribbean
MDG	Millennium Development Goal
MNA	Middle East and North Africa
MtCO$_2$e	megatons of carbon dioxide emissions
NDC	nationally determined contributions
PEFA	Public Expenditure and Financial Accountability
PIMI	Public Investment Management Index
PPI	private participation in infrastructure
PPP	public-private partnerships
RISE	Readiness for Investment in Sustainable Energy
SAIDI	System Average Interruption Duration Index

SAIFI	System Average Interruption Frequency Index
SDG	Sustainable Development Goal
SISBÉN	Sistema Nacional de Selección de Beneficiarios
SSA	Sub-Saharan Africa
PV	photovoltaic

Overview

Latin America and the Caribbean (henceforth referred to simply as Latin America) does not have the infrastructure it needs or deserves given its income level. Infrastructure also falls short of what is needed to advance social integration and achieve higher growth and prosperity. Moreover, the region's infrastructure does not correspond to the aspirations of its growing middle class.

Many argue that the solution is to spend more. With perhaps the exception of Africa, Latin America does invest the least in infrastructure among developing regions as a share of gross domestic product (GDP)—less than 3 percent compared with 4–7 percent elsewhere (table O.1). So the story might seem simple: the region underperforms on infrastructure and has to spend more to narrow its infrastructure "investment gap."

But that story would not match the facts.

First, the region's infrastructure performance varies, both across countries and sectors. The region invests little in infrastructure on average, but this average is driven by some of its largest countries: Argentina, Brazil, and Mexico. Many others—Bolivia, Costa Rica, Honduras, Nicaragua, Panama, Peru—invest more than 4 percent of GDP a year. Transport and wastewater are real challenges, but the region performs quite well in electricity and water. In fact, Latin America's clean, sophisticated electricity sector could become a serious competitive advantage.

Second, the focus should be on the *service* gap, rather than on a notional, and largely hypothetical, *investment* gap. To the question of, "How much is needed?" the response should always be: "For what?" And the answer should lie with countries' aspirations of economic growth and their social and environmental objectives, as well as with their choices as to the relative roles of infrastructure and other investments in achieving those aspirations.

Third, the investment gap approach necessarily focuses attention on the question of raising more resources. But closing the service gap should not—and, indeed, cannot—be just about spending more. The service gap can be narrowed, if not closed, in two other ways: by ensuring that spending (particularly of scarce public resources) is well targeted and that it is efficient.

This report has one main message: Latin America can dramatically narrow its infrastructure service gap by spending efficiently on the right things. It remains

Table O.1 Latin America Invests Little in Infrastructure, Compared to Other Developing Regions

Public and private infrastructure investments, latest year available

Region	Percentage of GDP
East Asia and the Pacific	5.8
Central Asia	4.0
Latin America and the Caribbean	2.8
Middle East and North Africa	6.9
South Asia	4.8
Sub-Saharan Africa	1.9

Source: http://Infralatam.info; ADB 2017; own estimates.
Note: GDP = gross domestic product. No data was available for Eastern Europe. Applying these shares to 2014 GDP figures suggests Latin America accounts for about $180 billion out of total developing country infrastructure spending of about $1.5 trillion.

to be seen whether spending better will be sufficient for the region to fully achieve what it aspires to. But there is sufficient evidence that spending better and focusing scarce public resources on what matters would significantly narrow the service gap.

The "spend better" message is also pragmatic. Most Latin American countries have limited fiscal space to increase public investments (total, not just infrastructure related); these have dropped to an average of about 3.4 percent of GDP across the region. Historically, only about a third of total public investment goes to infrastructure. So, at least in the short to medium term, it is highly unlikely that the region's public investment in infrastructure could rise much above 1.0–1.5 percent of GDP.

Could private investments be a way to close the service gap? Investments captured through the World Bank's private participation in infrastructure (PPI) database have ranged from 0.5 to 1.2 percent of GDP per year since 2006. But with about one-third of this financing coming from public sources, and about half of the deals requiring public guarantees, PPI expansion is constrained by limited public finance. In other words, while PPIs may help improve performance, they do not leverage significant amounts of private capital and are best seen as a complement to, rather than a substitute for, public investments.

As to commercial borrowing by public utilities, it is limited by poor creditworthiness, at least in the water sector: only 20 percent of the Latin American water utilities included in the International Benchmarking Network for Water and Sanitation Utilities (IBNET) database (2016) generate enough of a surplus to mobilize commercial borrowing (assumed to be cash revenues exceeding costs by at least 20 percent). This means that 80 percent of Latin America's water utilities would have difficulties in mobilizing commercial (nongovernment guaranteed) financing unless they implement significant reforms. Another way of looking at this is that greater efficiency could bring in much more financing (figure O.1).

So, realistically, Latin America is unlikely to see infrastructure investments rise much above 2.7 percent of GDP if it relies only on public spending and PPIs.

Figure O.1 With Greater Efficiency, Four Times as Many Water Utilities Could Access Private Financing
Percentage of utilities

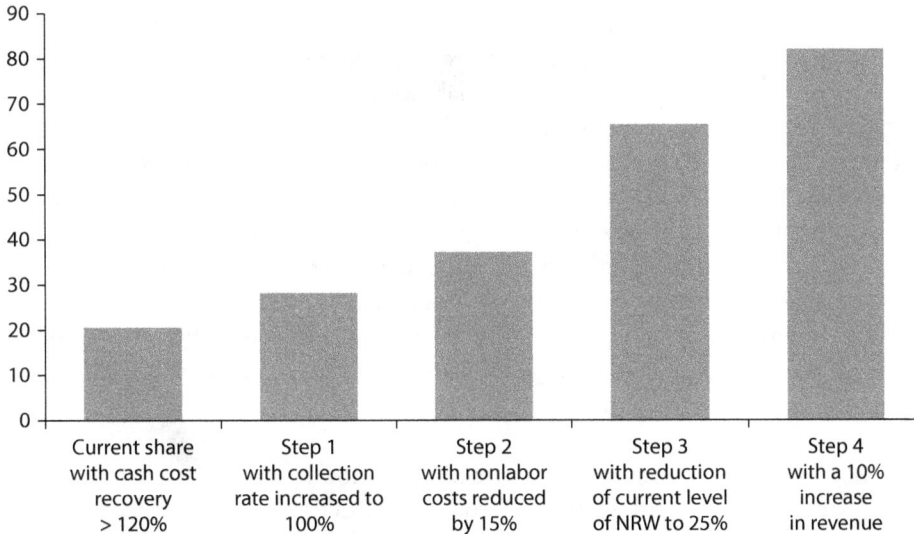

Source: Courtesy of William Kingdom and Alexander Danilenko (World Bank) based on IBNET database 2016.
Note: NRW = nonrevenue water, or water that is produced but "lost" before it reaches the consumer.

As such, spending better on the right things (which includes improving the creditworthiness of public utilities and the balance between user fees and taxpayer financing of infrastructure) is not just the best way to make a significant dent in the investment gap. For many countries it will be the only way.

Thus, this report advocates a much more careful discussion of investment needs in Latin America, one that starts with a debate about what infrastructure is needed given countries' development priorities (which typically also includes prudent fiscal policies), that thoroughly examines how to achieve infrastructure goals efficiently (which requires looking at country, sector, and project cost drivers), and that relies on well-thought-out rules of the game for deciding what should be financed by taxpayers rather than users.

As such, the key questions to ask are the following:

- What is the goal?
- How to achieve it as cost effectively as possible?
- Who pays?

The first two questions will determine investment needs, while the third will determine financing options. We address these three questions in what follows—hoping to offer a useful framework for countries to devise infrastructure strategies.

What Is the Goal? And How to Set It?

Infrastructure (defined here as power, water, sanitation, transport, flood protection, and the backbone of telecommunication) is necessary for growth, poverty alleviation, social inclusion, resilience, and environmental sustainability.

But it is the service that matters more than the kilometers of roads or pipes and cables, along with quality and affordability. In fact, better or more infrastructure is often only one of many ways to achieve a policy goal. Take transport as an example. If the objective is to improve mobility or access to services, it may be more effective to better regulate transport services or build more clinics and schools rather than roads and highways. And infrastructure needs change over time, as economies develop, societies urbanize, the middle class grows, the climate changes, and technologies drive transformation on many fronts.

Investment gap approaches seldom take these considerations into account. Instead, the methodologies behind the investment gap estimates do one of two things:

- They examine how infrastructure access or stocks have evolved historically relative to income, urbanization, economic structure, and other factors, then estimate what it would take to maintain this relationship. If in the past this access or stock was suboptimal, the projected ones will be as well. Importantly, *these estimates are in no way the result of an optimization exercise*: they do not represent the level of investment that will maximize growth or poverty reduction, but just what is needed for business as usual to continue.
- They price a goal (such as universal access to water or electricity) using either rough estimates of costs (such as average cost of a water connection) or, in best-case scenarios, an economic-engineering model (a least-cost optimization plan for the electricity network). This approach is useful where goals have been set (such as universal access to water or electricity) and can help inform policy debates by providing estimates of the costs of different goals (such as access to water or to safely managed water; in the house or within 100 meters of the dwelling) or different ways of achieving them. But it cannot substitute for policy choices regarding the service gap or public priorities—for example, in transport, where there is no simple "universal access" goal to aspire to.

So, how to think about Latin America's infrastructure goals? We suggest two sets of inputs that countries can factor in as they go about defining the infrastructure needed to support their economic, social, and environmental objectives. Again, however, these are no more than inputs to help make the needed policy choices.

Stocktaking along with Peer Comparison or Benchmarking—This Suggests That Latin America May Want to Focus on Sanitation and Transport

In comparing Latin America to its peers, there are clear areas of strength and weakness. The region scores well in terms of access to water and electricity.

Some 94 percent of households have access to improved water. The 20 million or so households that still lack access are concentrated in just six countries, and all but one (Haiti) are comfortably middle income, suggesting that full coverage is well within the region's financial capacity. The story is similar for electricity: 96 percent of households have access. Access rates are progressing well, helped by supportive policies (again with the exception of Haiti). Water and electricity utilities could do better, especially in terms of efficiency and cost recovery, but there are many good performers.

The electricity sector has the potential to turn into a great competitive advantage for the region. It is the cleanest of any region, based mostly on hydroelectricity. The increased uncertainty of water precipitation associated with climate change means that the region will need to diversify its renewable resources. It has significant potential in solar and wind, and while these remain just a sliver of overall generation, investments are increasing rapidly—not surprising in light of the high score given to the investment framework for renewables by World Bank analysis.

The policy framework for energy efficiency remains wanting, however, which results in poor electricity efficiency. This is a priority area, along with improving the regional connectivity of electricity systems. The region could potentially leapfrog into the kind of systems now emerging in high-income countries, with decentralized electricity production and consumers as "prosumers." Doing so would require a substantial evolution on the part of utilities, but the sophistication of the region's markets and regulators makes it a distinct possibility.

More challenging are sanitation and modern cooking fuels, both of which have serious implications for public health and human capital accumulation. Some 17 percent of Latin Americans have no access to a private, improved sanitation facility, and only about a third of wastewater is treated. The dismal wastewater performance is a real emergency, and one that epitomizes the potential for spending better. The sector is hampered by overly ambitious "imported" regulations that are unrealistic and leave no room for gradual improvement. Worse, legislation usually precludes resource recovery even though wastewater plants can be designed to generate electricity for their own use or sale, and gray water and treated sludge can be used for agriculture and other purposes. A case in point is Lima, a city of nearly 8.5 million in the middle of a desert, that discharges its used water into the ocean and disposes of its sludge in expensive sanitary landfills instead of allowing it to be used for agriculture.

As for modern cooking fuels, some 87 million people still lack access. This issue has not received sufficient attention or financial support. More than half the people of Guatemala, Honduras, and Nicaragua still use solid fuel for cooking, which results in serious public health implications. Even in relatively wealthy Mexico, the share is still 13 percent.

But the transport sector is where Latin America most underperforms its peers. This is partly due to the region's low population density, which makes it extremely hard to affordably develop a dense transport network. Latin America's paved road density is similar to that of Africa (as is the perception of its road quality, according to the World Economic Forum's rankings). This may be a normal consequence of the region's geography and need not imply that its countries need more roads. The region does have a very high road occupancy rate, however, as well as large pockets of inaccessibility.

Physical infrastructure is only part of the transportation challenge. A lack of competition in trucking and inefficient customs clearance processes are largely responsible for relatively low logistics performance. The road transport industry is some 15 times more concentrated than in the United States. In Central America, increased competition on national routes could reduce prices by 8 cents per ton-km as opposed to only 3 cents for tackling inefficiencies such as high congestion, long waits at borders, and bribery. The region has limited integration among different transport modes, especially rail and road. Ports suffer from highly congested access roads. In urban transport, a number of cities have modern, well-functioning bus rapid transit systems, but most struggle with high congestion, pockets of inaccessibility, inefficient and often inequitable pricing, and continuing reliance on informal public transport providers.

Emerging Needs and Challenges: Climate Change, Increased Demand, and Urbanization

Infrastructure is typically long lived and influences households and firms' own investments and locational choices—choices that are difficult to reverse, creating lock-ins. As such, infrastructure decisions need to be forward looking. Two trends that matter for the region's infrastructure choices are climate change and the combination of urbanization and changing socioeconomics.

Climate change means that energy, transport, and water and sanitation systems will need to be built differently to become more resilient to extreme events and better able to respond to associated changes in demand: more electricity during heat waves, better water storage to cope with both droughts and extreme rains, and protective dams and improved drainage to reduce flood risk.

Climate change will also increase the need for better resource management—it is another factor that creates pressure for greater efficiency, especially for water and energy. Mexico, and to a lesser extent Brazil and Colombia, have policies in place to boost energy efficiency. But implementation has been weak and has occurred mostly in the context of domestic energy crises. Further, fossil fuel subsidies remain high in countries such as Argentina, Bolivia, Chile, Ecuador, and República Bolivariana de Venezuela. In general, the region has significant potential for improving energy efficiency.

Climate change also means that pressures will mount to reduce emissions from infrastructure. As mentioned above, this could become a source of comparative advantage for Latin America, which has the cleanest electricity matrix in the world. But increasingly variable precipitation and strong popular pushback against dams are making it increasingly urgent for the region to diversify its renewable energy sources. Transport emissions are growing rapidly, and without action, emissions from infrastructure-related sectors are likely to increase further.

A business-as-usual scenario, with increased motorization and decreased reliance on hydroelectricity, would see energy-related emissions more than double across the region between 2010 and 2050.

Changing socioeconomics are also affecting the demand for infrastructure services. The region's middle class grew by about 50 percent during the boom years of 2003–09. The vast majority of the middle class has access to basic services but is far from saturated in terms of consumer durables (notably cars, air conditioners, and washing machines). The combination of higher incomes with a recent boom in consumer credit could significantly raise overall energy demand, in a way that may not be sufficiently taken into account in traditional energy forecasts. At the same time, most remaining challenges in basic access to water and electricity are now concentrated among the poorest decile, which may be the social group most difficult to reach, either because of remoteness or depth of poverty. The last-mile challenge may well be more complex than previous ones and require innovation in technology, delivery, and financing.

Linked with changing socioeconomics is the region's ongoing but changing urbanization. Density has declined in Brasilia, Buenos Aires, La Paz, Montevideo, and Santiago, driven by transport, land use, and housing policies. If expansion patterns continue unchanged, built-up urban areas could double in the region by 2035, pushing up infrastructure costs. A recent World Bank review of urbanization in Mexico suggests that denser urbanization would reduce infrastructure investments and maintenance costs by 41 percent in Merida and 67 percent in Los Cabos.

Another critical question is whether the region can improve how urbanization is planned and managed. Unplanned urban expansion translates into higher costs as slum upgrading costs two to eight times more than regular land development. Already some 25 percent of the region's urban dwellers live in slums, and they account for a large claim on the region's infrastructure investment budget.

How to Improve Services as Cost-Effectively as Possible?

Spending better could materially reduce the cost of improving infrastructure in Latin America. Take the case of electricity: availability can be increased by building more power plants or by improving energy efficiency. And despite having a rather sophisticated and mature electricity market, the region still fares poorly on energy efficiency. In fact, transmission and distribution losses are some of the highest in the world. Not surprisingly, background work done for this report finds that electricity investment needs would average US$23 billion to US$24 billion a year if South America follows the same investment path it has in the past, but perhaps as little as US$8 billion to US$9 billion if it adopts a transformational approach that favors demand-side management, energy efficiency, and renewable energy solutions. (This number only includes investments and not the cost of demand-side management and energy efficiency programs. The total would be higher, but still likely to be substantially less than under a traditional path.)

Rethinking Infrastructure in Latin America and the Caribbean
http://dx.doi.org/10.1596/978-1-4648-1101-2

Similarly, for water, the World Bank estimates that the Sustainable Development Goal of universal access to safely managed water and sanitation would cost between 0.1 and 0.4 percent of GDP a year through 2030, depending on how it is implemented. A reasonable way forward would cost about 0.25 percent of GDP—roughly what the region has been investing in recent years, with good results on water but less so on sanitation.

A simple framework is useful to think through the various elements of reform needed to improve infrastructure spending efficiency. The ultimate objective is to deliver infrastructure services to households and firms in a way that maximizes some measure of welfare. Hence it will depend

- on the supply side, on the cost of producing such services, from the initial construction of supporting networks to the end delivery of services to users, and
- on the demand side, on the availability and affordability of services, given the quality produced and the pricing schemes for users.

On the supply side, key whole-of-government challenges have been identified as particularly problematic for public investment management. These include the following:

- *Weak planning, project appraisal, and preparation capacity.* Work by the World Bank, Inter-American Development Bank, and International Monetary Fund shows that Latin America has a low level of investment efficiency, with the weakest stages of public investment management being appraisal and evaluation. Many projects are funded that are not sufficiently prepared—either because of limited capacity or oversight, or because of parliamentary amendments to annual budget laws. This is a serious issue in Brazil in particular, where a combination of weak capacity, lax enforcement, and pork-barrel politics results in investment projects being included in ministerial budgets without having been subject to formal appraisal.

- *Overly rigid or myopic budgeting.* This is designed to manage fiscal deficits and focuses on controlling cash expenditures rather than promoting efficient spending. As a result, most countries have annual budgets that do not allow for carryover. This results in rushed procurement and execution and is further complicated by the fact that the fiscal year runs from January to December, when the right time for public works in most countries is the dry season of November to March. Colombia appears to be one of the few countries in the region that has a strong planning system and that has introduced medium-term expenditures frameworks. Other countries have created fiduciary funds to avoid this budget rigidity, choose public-private partnerships (PPPs), or continue to cope with multiannual allocations.

- *Difficulties with budget execution.* This is a particular issue in Brazil, where disbursement data show a chronic gap between committed and executed funds (figure O.2).

Figure O.2 Many Latin American Countries Chronically Underexecute Their Capital Investment Budget
Disbursement as percentage of commitment

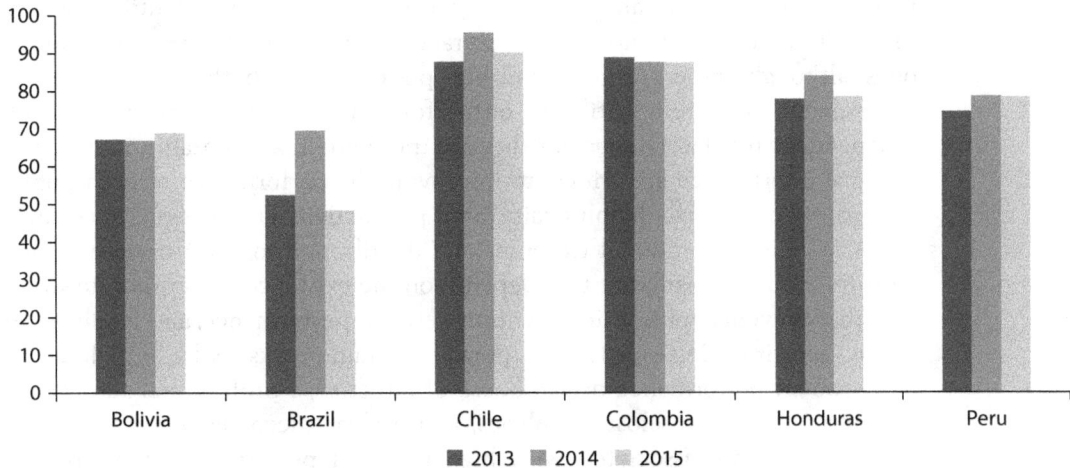

Source: Courtesy of Diego Dorado, based on data from government budgetary reporting systems.

- *Procurement that could be improved.* Inefficient procurement processes contribute to limited budget execution and excess costs. Some countries in the region such as Chile and Mexico have seen remarkable success in driving procurement reforms. For example, the ChileCompra electronic portal is estimated to have generated US$280 million in savings. Mexico's modernization of its tendering processes generated savings of more than US$1 billion within three years of its 2009 start. But a detailed analysis of procurement performance across the region shows that there is considerable room for improvement. The World Bank's *Benchmarking Public Procurement 2017* report found that suppliers identify obstacles such as excessive bureaucracy and red tape in Colombia and Honduras; payment delays in Argentina, the Dominican Republic, and Jamaica; lack of transparency and opaque tendering processes in Brazil and Mexico; and inefficiency in Barbados.

- *Unclear project sustainability.* This can be caused by an imbalance between capital and current spending on infrastructure. This can spring from overly rigid budgets and suboptimal planning—very few countries in the region link investment budgets and forward expenditure estimates—or from poor coordination between central governments (which fund and often manage capital investments) and local governments (which may lack the financial and technical capacity to take over these investments or cover operation and maintenance costs).

- *An uncompetitive construction industry.* Competition policy, to the extent that it affects competition in construction and related activities, is likely to have an important impact on construction costs.

Rethinking Infrastructure in Latin America and the Caribbean
http://dx.doi.org/10.1596/978-1-4648-1101-2

Next comes a postconstruction stage that relates to operational efficiency in service delivery and depends on the ownership structure, the quality of the regulatory framework, and corporate governance. A review of utility performance in the region found that, on average, private utilities outperform public ones, although there are good and bad performers in both groups (the top 10 percent of public utilities outperform the average private utility). Independent regulatory agencies that are transparent, accountable, and free of political interference are critical to improving the performance of both public and private operators—helping raise labor productivity and cost-recovery ratios while reducing operational expenses and distribution losses. For state-owned enterprises, performance further depends on the existence of a corporate structure that prevents political intervention, rewards performance, and is subject to public scrutiny. Best-practice corporatized frameworks—which include an independent performance-driven board of directors, a professional staff, transparency and clear disclosure policies, and a clear mechanism for evaluating performance—are associated with high levels of performance, with performance orientation and professional management being the most important contributors.

Similarly, for transport (the one nonutility sector we examine), substantial efficiency gains are likely to come from regulatory frameworks that encourage both greater intermodal coordination and more competition in the industries related to transport services. The latter may allow for substantial gains to be redirected from profits in these industries to consumers of infrastructure. For example, monopolistic freight transport services may well end up capturing most of the potential rent created by additional physical infrastructure, reducing demand and potentially nullifying the gain from the investments.

Finally, on the demand side, a number of price-related aspects are key to driving efficiency. The first is simply adequate pricing, which encourages efficient use by consumers (to buy more fuel-efficient cars, use public transportation, turn off lights, buy energy-efficient appliances, fix leaking faucets, and so on). Pricing services appropriately also makes it possible to attract commercial financing, which in turn may create additional pressures for efficiency.

But adequate pricing is not simply cost-recovery tariffs. It needs to factor in social acceptability—which requires that price regulation go hand in hand with regulation of quality and with considerations of availability and affordability. This last point is where equity concerns and issues of externalities should be included, to ensure that policy makers consider the added social value of services (for example, in water, sanitation, or public transport) when defining what should be funded by taxpayers rather than users.

But while pricing is important, other mechanisms (incentives, information, and nudges such as options that default to more efficient settings, quotas, or performance standards) are available to push consumers to switch to more efficient patterns of consumption and appliances. These can be helpful complements, especially where price elasticities are low.

Who Should Pay—And What Does It Imply in Terms of Financing Options?

Spending efficiently on the right things also means making judicious use of scarce public resources. Infrastructure is funded by either taxpayers or users. Taxpayer money is best used where it is not possible to charge the users (as with flood protection or rural roads) or not desirable to do so (because of environmental and social externalities that result in underconsumption of the service, as with water treatment or public transportation, or due to equity concerns as in subsidies targeting the poor).

But the potential for cost recovery cannot be divorced from the efficiency with which a service is provided. Poor quality service will reduce willingness to pay, while high costs will reduce the likelihood of achieving full cost recovery, especially if there is a perception of inefficiency or predatory pricing on the part of the service provider. And even where subsidies may be justified by externalities, as with wastewater treatment for example, it may be possible to reduce the needed subsidies by reducing costs. Most countries find it difficult to achieve full cost recovery for wastewater treatment plants using traditional business models, under which a water treatment plant is a cost center. Instead, new models are being proposed whereby water treatment plants can generate electricity for self-consumption and even sale to the network and can sell sanitized sludge for use as a fertilizer.

Charging users, where possible and appropriate, has a number of advantages. First, it helps manage demand. Second, it creates a market test and puts pressure on the service provider (public or private) to improve quality. Indeed, there is some evidence that the efficiency gains typically associated with PPI are dependent on such a market test. (This raises some concerns, given that only about 43 percent of the region's PPPs are backed by user fees or a purchasing agreement with fully private utilities.) Third, charging users directly increases the revenue base for investments and creates the potential for commercial financing, regardless of who operates or owns the infrastructure. And commercial financing in turn is likely to create pressure for greater efficiency.

In this context, the World Bank Group, along with other multilateral development banks, is suggesting an approach that weighs the benefits and opportunity costs of deploying public and/or concessional resources (figure O.3). The starting point of this approach is that any investment project or program that *can* be financed on commercial terms while remaining affordable and offering value for money, *should be.*

Where commercial financing is not cost effective or viable due to perceived risks or market failures, efforts should focus on addressing these market failures through upstream reforms to strengthen country and sector policies, regulations, and institutions or with targeted public interventions (for example, targeted subsidies or complementary public investments, such as transmission lines). Where risks remain high and raise the cost of commercial capital beyond that afforded by project or corporate revenue generation, it may be possible to reduce costs through risk-sharing instruments backed by public or concessional finance.

Figure O.3 A Decision-Making Framework to Ensure the Judicious Use of Scarce Public and Concessional Finance

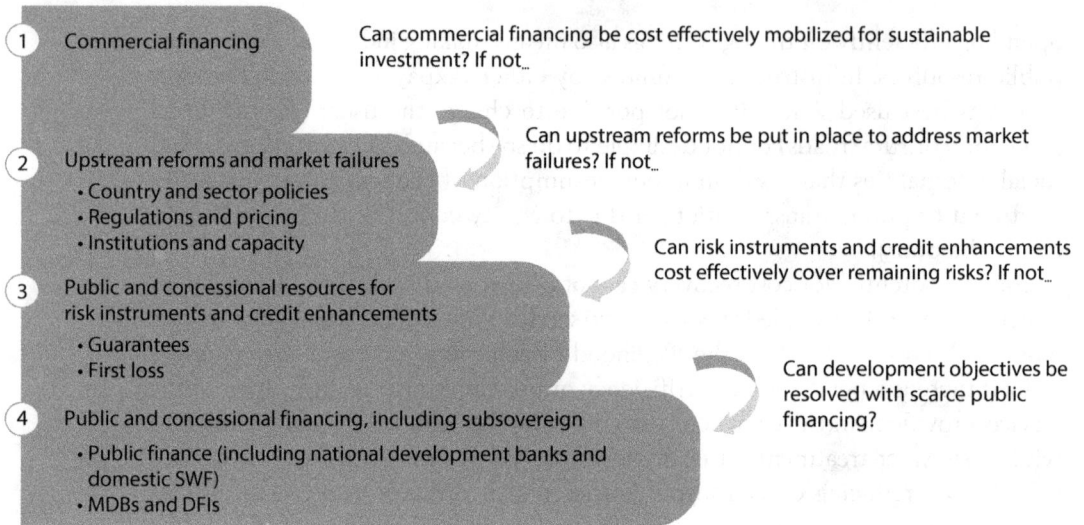

① Commercial financing

Can commercial financing be cost effectively mobilized for sustainable investment? If not...

② Upstream reforms and market failures
  • Country and sector policies
  • Regulations and pricing
  • Institutions and capacity

Can upstream reforms be put in place to address market failures? If not...

③ Public and concessional resources for risk instruments and credit enhancements
  • Guarantees
  • First loss

Can risk instruments and credit enhancements cost effectively cover remaining risks? If not...

④ Public and concessional financing, including subsovereign
  • Public finance (including national development banks and domestic SWF)
  • MDBs and DFIs

Can development objectives be resolved with scarce public financing?

Source: World Bank 2017.
Note: DFI = Development Finance Institution; MDB = Multilateral Development Bank; SWF = Sovereign Wealth Fund.

Only where commercial financing is still not viable or cost effective should public and concessional resources be deployed.

Importantly, this framework can only be applied to services that can be charged to users, as user fees are what creates the basis for commercial financing options beyond the use of general taxes.[1]

Equity and poverty concerns are not at odds with reliance on commercial financing, even though they are often invoked in arguments against full cost recovery for basic services such as water and sanitation, electricity, public transport, and modern cooking fuels. The needs of the poor are in fact typically best served by a combination of cost-recovery tariffs and targeted subsidies and payments schemes adapted to their needs. Most of the wealthier Latin American countries have well-developed social registries and safety nets (for example, Brazil, Chile, Colombia, Mexico), but targeting is likely to be a challenge for countries without these in place.

Conclusions

Latin America spends a good deal of money on infrastructure. In return, it gets the following:

• High electricity access—with good prospects for closing the access gap given that the remaining unconnected households are concentrated in mostly middle-income countries—but low nonsolid fuel access, with serious health implications

- The world's cleanest electricity—mostly from hydroelectricity, which is challenged by increasingly frequent droughts—and small but rapidly growing wind and solar sectors
- Some world-class utilities for both water and electricity, and a few countries with sophisticated, stable, and predictable regulations, especially for electricity. But most utilities and regulatory schemes could do better, with potentially significant cost and resource savings
- Relatively high water access, though quality and safety remain poor, with sewerage access low and less than 30 percent of wastewater being treated—an unacceptable level for a region with its levels of income and urbanization
- Mediocre transport services because of poor infrastructure and an uncompetitive transport industry, resulting in costly freight transport, congested cities, and deep pockets of rural isolation

Improving the region's infrastructure performance in a context of tight fiscal space will require spending better on well-identified priorities. Unlike most infrastructure diagnostics, this report insists that much of what is needed lies outside the infrastructure sector and has to do with broader government issues—from competition policy to budgeting rules that no longer solely focus on controlling cash expenditures. But quite a lot also involves sector reforms, with the traditional recommendations regarding independent, well-performing regulators and better corporate governance continuing to apply. We also insist on the critical importance of cost recovery where feasible and desirable, since user fees are the basis for commercial finance—while keeping in mind the importance of reducing costs, either through efficiency or adoption of alternative business models, such as those emerging for water treatment plants.

Latin America has long been an innovator in infrastructure. The report notes many challenges, but it also highlights many examples of the region's capacity for innovative solutions, its expertise with sophisticated regulations, and its experience with PPPs. Latin America has the means and potential to do better. And it can do so by spending more efficiently on the right things.

Note

1. In addition, there may be potential to capture the value created through infrastructure investments in less traditional ways (land-value capture, congestion charging, parking fees) or through the commercial exploitation of infrastructure assets (advertising, real estate).

References

ADB (Asian Development Bank). 2017. "Meeting Asia's Infrastructure Needs." Manila: ADB.

World Bank. 2017. "Infrastructure Finance: Guiding Principles for the World Bank Group–A Cascade Decision-Making Approach." World Bank, Washington, DC.

Infrastructure in Latin America and the Caribbean: Modest Spending, Uneven Results

Infrastructure serves a number of purposes. It provides the underlying conditions for increased development, be it by providing more efficient transport, the last-mile water supply for the poor, or energy for all. It can serve to reduce inequalities (by serving slum dwellers rather than favoring better off residents of cities), it can open access to markets to increase prosperity (transport infrastructure), and it is recognized as a core input into any sustainable growth strategy.

So what should Latin America and the Caribbean be spending on infrastructure?[1] Estimates vary widely—from 3 to 8 percent of regional gross domestic product (GDP)—though they tend to hover around 4 to 5 percent. Most of these estimates use a simplistic methodology that measures only how infrastructure spending would need to evolve as it has historically, along with economic growth (box 1.1). They do not indicate what Latin America should be spending to maximize growth (though some studies look at the cost of achieving a specific social, economic, or environmental goal). Such estimates are the results of benchmarking exercises, not optimization exercises.

Yet there is widespread agreement in policy circles and in the news media that Latin America needs to spend more on infrastructure. This belief comes from general dissatisfaction with infrastructure services in the region and the widely held idea that increased spending on infrastructure is key to improving the region's growth and competitiveness.

But would increased spending solve Latin America's infrastructure challenges? To start answering that question, this section examines how much Latin America currently spends on infrastructure—from both public and private sources—and what it gets for its money.

What we find, on average, is modest spending and uneven results across sectors and countries. The region has made impressive progress in some areas, such as extending access to water and developing modern public transport systems in

---

Box 1.1 How Should Latin America Define Its Needs for Infrastructure Investment?

Fay (2001) and Fay and Yepes (2003) provided the first estimates of infrastructure investment needs in developing regions. Their approach was essentially a benchmarking one, using simple econometrics to examine how infrastructure spending has evolved over time along with income, population, urbanization, gross domestic product (GDP) composition, and other relevant determinants of household and firm demand for infrastructure services. It then priced the investment needed to keep pace with increases in income, population, and urbanization.

The main limitation of this approach is that there is no optimization. It simply prices what it would take to maintain the historically observed (possibly constrained) relation between infrastructure and income, population, and urbanization. The approach does not establish a causal relationship between investments and growth, nor does it price a specific desired objective (such as the Millennium or Sustainable Development Goals). It is also very sensitive to assumptions about future growth rates.

Subsequent authors (Kohli and Basil 2011; Perrotti and Sánchez 2011; Ruiz-Nuñez and Wei 2015) have introduced various improvements and updates to this original model, with estimates for Latin America ranging from 3.6 to 6.0 percent of the region's GDP (table B1.1.1). To our knowledge, however, no one has been able to answer the question of optimality (the amount of investment needed to achieve a particular growth path). CAF (2011), Powell (2013), and Serebrisky and others (2015) mostly draw from this body of work to conclude that the region's infrastructure investment needs are 4–6 percent of GDP.

Climate change considerations have also affected estimates and methodologies. Bhattacharya, Romani, and Stern (2012) estimate that Latin America would need an additional US$200 billion to US$300 billion a year to achieve mitigation and resilience objectives. But whereas reasonable methodologies exist to estimate the cost of low-carbon investment pathways, estimating adaptation investment needs at the level of a country—let alone a region—is pure guesswork.

Table B1.1.1 Estimated Annual Spending Requirements for Infrastructure in Latin America Vary Considerably

Authors	Estimates (percentage of GDP)	Period of prediction	Maintenance included? (percentage of GDP if provided)
Fay and Morrison (2007)[a]	4.0–6.0	2010–30	Yes (1.0)
Fay and Morrison (2007)[b]	3.0	2010–20	Yes (1.0)
Perrotti and Sánchez (2011)	5.2	2006–20	Yes (2.5)
Kohli and Basil (2011)	4.0	2011–40	Yes
Ruiz-Nuñez and Wei (2015)	3.6	2014–20	Yes (1.8)
CAF (2011)	5.0–6.0	2010–40	Yes
Bhattacharya, Romani, and Stern (2012)	6.0–8.0	2012–20	No

Note: GDP = gross domestic product.
a. Level of investment needed to bring Latin America's infrastructure to a level equivalent to that of the Republic of Korea.
b. Level of investment needed given expected growth and historical co-evolution of infrastructure, GPD, and economic structure, plus cost of achieving universal coverage in water, sanitation, and electricity.

many large cities. Some water and energy utilities are world class. But too many Latin Americans still suffer from poor or nonexistent services. The region is far from having the infrastructure it needs to compete internationally and provide the middle-class standard of living that many of its people aspire to and that a mostly upper-middle-income region should be able to deliver.

How Much Does Latin America Spend on Infrastructure?

During 2008–13 (the most recent years for which data are available), average annual investment in infrastructure in Latin American ranged from 2.4 to 3.2 percent of GDP, for an average of 2.7 percent (figure 1.1). This is far from the upper-bound "needs" estimates of 8 percent, or even from the 4–5 percent average suggested in table B1.1.1, but in line with the lower-bound estimate of 3 percent.

This regional average masks large differences across countries, from 1.6 percent of GDP in Mexico to 6 percent in Nicaragua (figure 1.2). Indeed, the average is largely determined by Argentina, Brazil, and Mexico, which together account for four-fifths of the region's GDP.[2] Many other countries—such as Bolivia, Costa Rica, Panama, and Peru—invested more than 4 percent. No pattern emerges about country size or income level. For example, smaller, poorer Central American countries are evenly split between those that invested a little (El Salvador, Guatemala) and those that invested a lot (Honduras, Nicaragua).

Public-private partnerships (PPPs) accounted for some 40 percent of the region's infrastructure investments—though with significant variation, from

Figure 1.1 Public and Private Infrastructure Investments in Latin America Have Been Fairly Stable, 2008–13

Percentage of GDP

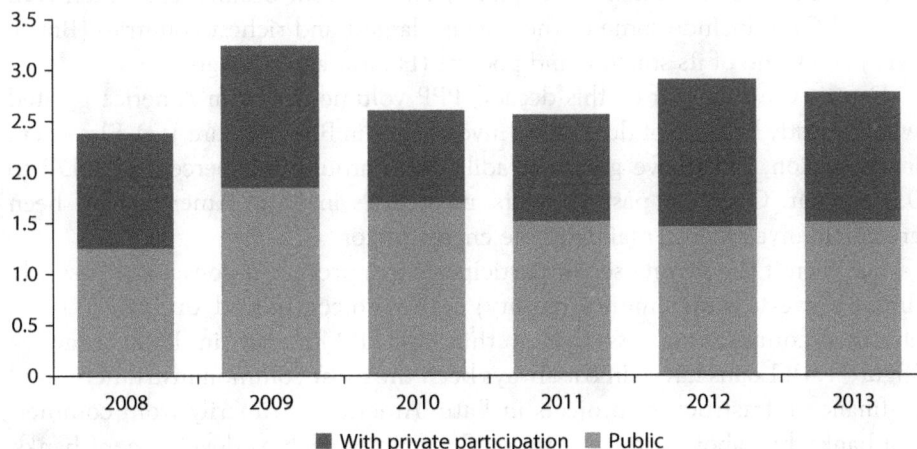

■ With private participation　■ Public

Source: http://www.infralatam.info, downloaded on August 4, 2016.
Note: GDP = gross domestic product. Includes investments in electricity, telecommunications, transport, and water and sanitation. Data weighted by country GDP. Data on investments with private participation come from World Bank Private Participation in Infrastructure Database (http://www.ppi.worldbank.org), represent committed rather than actual investments, and are reported in full for the year they are committed rather than when investments are disbursed.

Figure 1.2 Infrastructure Investment Levels Varied Enormously across Countries, 2008–13
Percentage of GDP

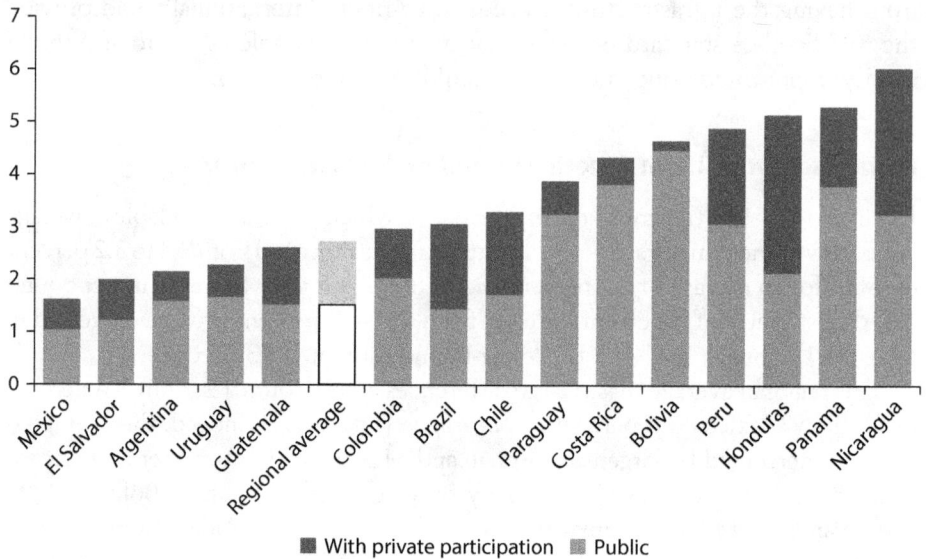

Source: http://www.infralatam.info, downloaded on May 2, 2016.
Note: GDP = gross domestic product. See figure 1.1.

4 percent in Bolivia to 58 percent in Honduras, again with no clear pattern on the basis of country size or income. (A note of caution is in order in interpreting these numbers as these are commitments rather than actual investments. Moreover, they are recorded in full the year a deal is signed, rather than spread over time as the investments take place.) The top four destinations in terms of share of GDP include some of the region's largest and richest countries (Brazil, Peru) and some of its smallest and poorest (Honduras, Nicaragua).

During the first half of this decade, PPP volumes in Latin America gyrated wildly, mostly because of fluctuating investments in Brazil (figure 1.3). Elsewhere in the region, PPPs have grown steadily, from around 0.2 percent of GDP to 0.8 percent. Over the past 10 years, most PPPs in Latin America have been greenfield investments, mainly in the energy sector.

But even if the private sector participates in a project, it does not necessarily directly invest its own money (equity) in the project. Indeed, during 2011–15, equity accounted for less than a third of PPP finance in Latin America (figure 1.4). Loans have almost always been the most common instrument used to finance infrastructure projects in Latin America—primarily from commercial banks, but about a third from public sources such as development banks, state and national banks, export credit agencies, and other public authorities and companies.[3] Bonds remain a small share (12 percent on average over the past five years) even though the region leads emerging economies in the use of bonds for infrastructure financing.

Figure 1.3 Infrastructure Public-Private Partnership Commitments Have Fluctuated Wildly in Latin America, 1990–2015

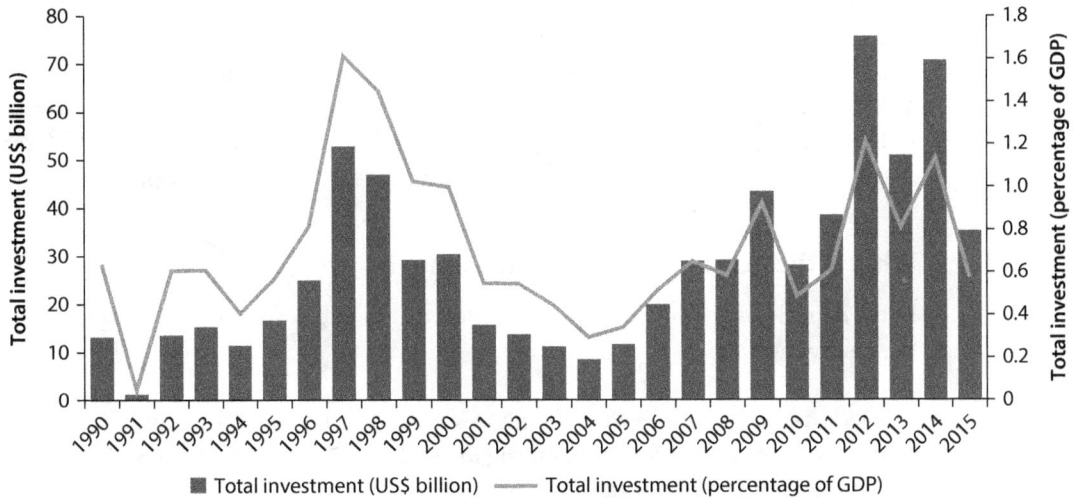

Source: Private Participation in Infrastructure Database, https://ppi.worldbank.org, downloaded April 15, 2016.
Note: GDP = gross domestic product. Data represent committed rather than actual investments and are reported in full for the year they are committed rather than when investments are disbursed.

Figure 1.4 Equity Accounts for a Small Share of Public Partnership Finance in Latin America, 2000–15
US$ billions

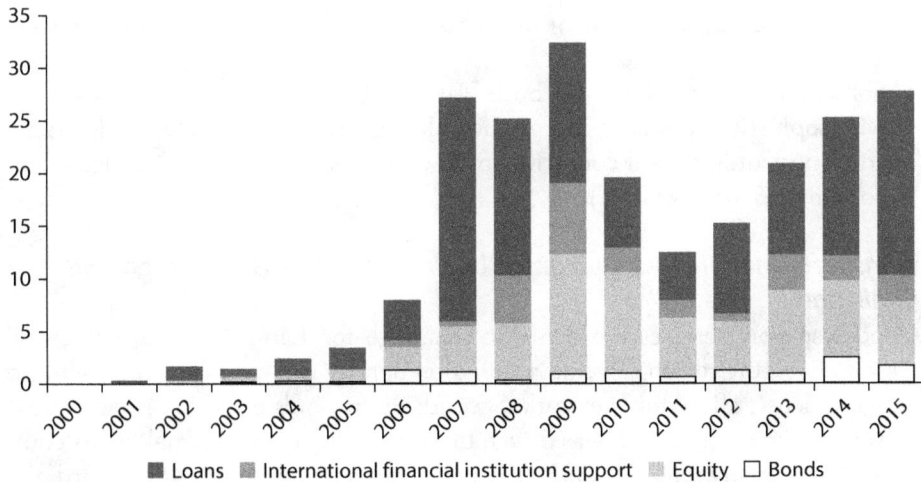

Source: Project Finance and Infrastructure Journal, http://www.ijglobal.com, downloaded May 5, 2016.

More generally, direct and indirect government support plays a critical role in facilitating private investment in infrastructure.[4] From 2010 to 2014, about half of all PPP deals in Latin America received some form of government support through direct or indirect contributions, with payment guarantees being the most common type of support. The energy sector got the highest share of guarantees, while transport received the highest share of direct government support.

Government support typically declines with the maturity of the PPP market, but it does not disappear: in 2000–14, nearly 75 percent of PPPs in countries with limited experience with such projects received guarantees, compared with 45 percent of PPPs in countries with stronger track records. These direct and indirect guarantees create contingent liabilities for the public sector even if there is still debate on how they should be accounted for in public accounts.

What Is the Region Getting for Its Money?

Latin America spends a fair bit of money on infrastructure. In exchange, it gets the following:

- Mediocre transport services owing to low-quality infrastructure and an uncompetitive transport industry resulting in costly freight transport, congested cities, and deep pockets of rural isolation
- Relatively high water access, though quality and safety remain poor given that sewerage coverage is low and less than 30 percent of wastewater is treated—an unacceptable level for a region with its levels of income and urbanization
- High electricity access, with the remaining unconnected areas concentrated in a few countries (rich and poor) and good prospects for closing the access gap, but low access to nonsolid fuel—with serious health implications
- The world's cleanest electricity, mostly from hydroelectricity (though threatened by increasingly frequent droughts), and small but rapidly growing solar and wind sectors
- Some world-class utilities for both water and electricity and a few countries with sophisticated, stable, and predictable regulations, especially for electricity (But most utilities and countries could do better, potentially with significant cost and resource savings.)

Transport: Unimpressive Outcomes, but Infrastructure Is Just Part of the Challenge

Good transport services are a major challenge for Latin America for several reasons. First, the region's overall population density is low, making it difficult to design a dense, affordable network. Second, the region's economy is dependent on trade—the recent boom was driven by commodity exports—making its competitiveness highly sensitive to the performance of its transport sector. Third, the region's high urbanization and relatively high income call for fairly sophisticated urban transport systems.

Rising awareness of the implications of poor transport infrastructure likely explains the substantial increase in transport investments between 2002 and 2013. These started to pick up in 2004 and grew significantly through 2009, hovering around 1.00–1.25 percent of GDP since 2007, more than other infrastructure sectors (figure 1.5, panel a). But trends varied by country. Most larger, richer

Figure 1.5 Downs and Ups in Transport Investments in Latin America, 2000–13
Percentage of GDP

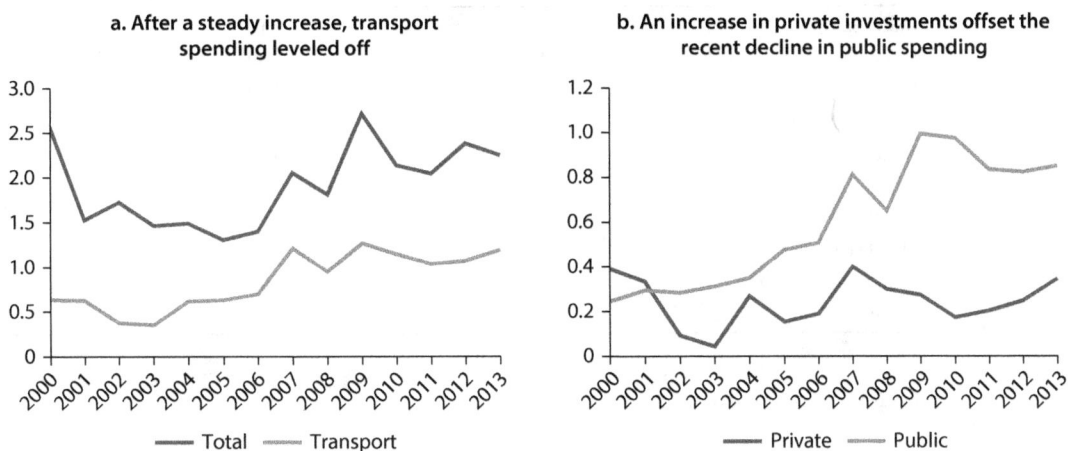

a. After a steady increase, transport spending leveled off

b. An increase in private investments offset the recent decline in public spending

— Total ⋯⋯ Transport

— Private ⋯⋯ Public

Source: Infralatam, http://www.infralatam.info, downloaded on November 15, 2016.

countries (Argentina, Brazil, Mexico) spent around 1 percent of GDP during 2008–13, while others (Bolivia, Nicaragua, Panama, Peru) spent two to three times as much. Public investments dominated the period, though a recent increase in private investment helped offset a drop in public spending (figure 1.5, panel b).

Weak Infrastructure and an Uncompetitive Industry Result in Poor Performance

Despite increased investment, transport performance remains poor. Latin America has low transport infrastructure density given its income level, with paved road density similar to Africa's and about one-quarter that of the next lowest region (table 1.1). This may, however, be a normal consequence of the region's geography and need not necessarily imply that the region needs more roads. Nevertheless, Latin America's roadway occupancy rate is higher than that of any other region (figure 1.6), and the region is characterized by a combination of large pockets of inaccessibility and congestion challenges, particularly in large cities. For rail infrastructure, density is less than 5 kilometers per thousand square kilometers for countries with a rail network compared with 16 kilometers per thousand square kilometers for Organisation for Economic Co-operation and Development (OECD) countries. More relevant is the fact that service is limited and not an effective substitute for, or even complement to, road transport. Only Brazil and Mexico carry more than 20 percent of freight by rail (CAF 2013).

Moreover, the region's infrastructure is perceived as being of rather low quality. Road, rail, port, and air infrastructure improved steadily in Eastern Europe and Central Asia over the past 10 years, but in Latin America, roads and ports improved only marginally, and railroads and airports did not improve at all (figure 1.7). In 2016, international investors ranked the region's road infrastructure at the same level as that of Sub-Saharan Africa. Argentina, Brazil, Colombia,

Table 1.1 Road Density in Latin America Is Lower than almost Anywhere Else, 2010

	2010 density level (paved lane-km per km² land)
OECD Europe	2.10
India	1.30
China	0.70
OECD North America	0.50
OECD Pacific	0.40
Japan	5.50
ASEAN	0.40
Middle East	0.20
Latin America	0.05
Africa	0.04

Source: Dulac 2013.

Note: ASEAN = Association of Southeast Asian Nations; km = kilometer; km² = square kilometer; OECD = Organisation for Economic Co-operation and Development.

Figure 1.6 Latin America Has the World's Highest Road Occupancy Levels, 2000–10

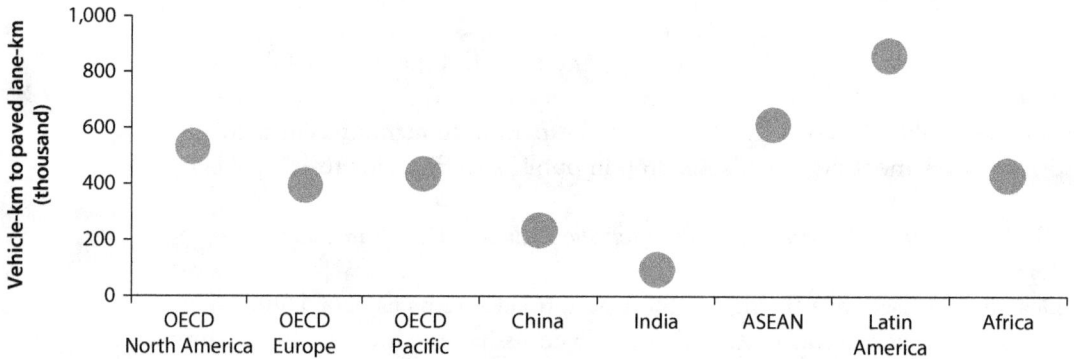

Source: Dulac 2013.

Note: ASEAN = Association of Southeast Asian Nations; km = kilometer; OECD = Organisation for Economic Co-operation and Development. Bubble sizes indicate average annual vehicle travel between 2000 and 2010.

Costa Rica, Paraguay, Peru, and Uruguay have particularly low rankings given their income levels.

Latin American airports, historically superior to those of other emerging economies, have fallen behind (see figure 1.7, panel d). Passenger demand has risen in recent years, powered by the continued emergence of a Latin American middle class—a trend expected to continue. In freight, Latin America/Europe and Latin America/North America routes have been growing steadily and are expected to continue to grow by about 5 percent a year over the next decade (Crabtree and others 2015). Turnaround costs for planes rose 34 percent in real terms over the period 1995–2009, more than in most North American and European airports (Serebrisky 2011).

Ports appear to have improved somewhat over the past decade—as measured both by liner shipping connectivity (an index that captures how well countries are connected to global shipping networks) and by international investors'

Figure 1.7 International Investors Are Not Impressed with Latin America's Transport Infrastructure, 2006–16

Logistics Performance Index, 1 = worst, 7 = best

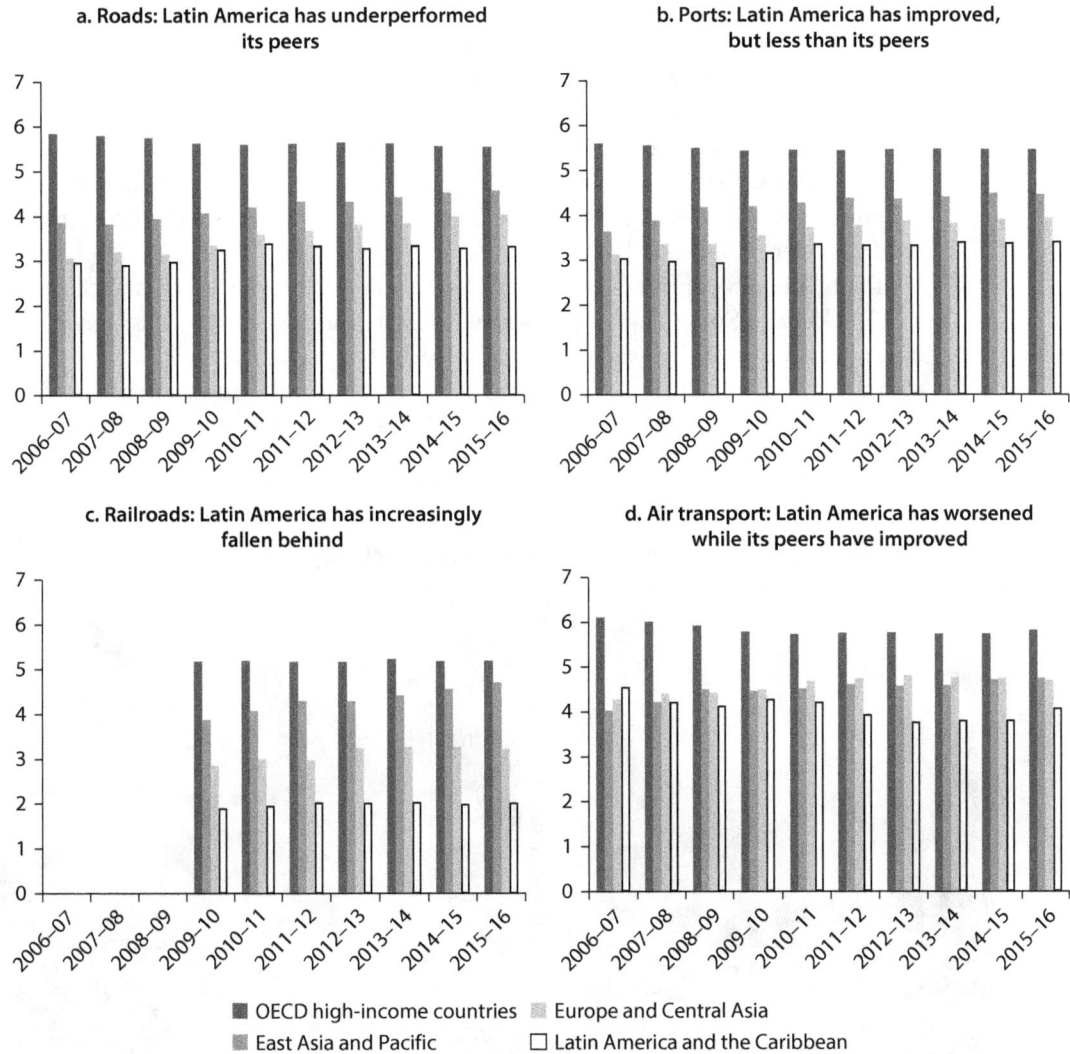

a. Roads: Latin America has underperformed its peers

b. Ports: Latin America has improved, but less than its peers

c. Railroads: Latin America has increasingly fallen behind

d. Air transport: Latin America has worsened while its peers have improved

■ OECD high-income countries ▓ Europe and Central Asia
▓ East Asia and Pacific □ Latin America and the Caribbean

Source: WEF 2015.
Note: OECD = Organisation for Economic Co-operation and Development. Country scores weighted by gross domestic product (in constant 2010 US$) to calculate regional aggregates. High-income countries excluded from regional aggregates.

impressions—but by less than the region's peers (figure 1.7, panel b). A particular challenge for ports is access infrastructure: surface infrastructure such as access roads would need to increase by some 15 percent within 50 kilometers of ports and key transport centers by 2030 given current and predicted trade volumes (ITF 2016).

The effects of generally poor infrastructure are compounded by an uncompetitive road transport industry that is some 15 times more concentrated than that of the United States (OECD and ECLAC 2012). Data for Argentina, Brazil, Colombia, Costa Rica, El Salvador, Guatemala, Mexico, and Paraguay suggest that 44 percent of road hauls in these countries are made without fee-earning return journeys—a sure way to increase costs and congestion (IDB 2015). In Central America, improved cost efficiencies—offsetting or reducing the effects of congestion, long wait times at borders, and high informal payments—could cut costs by 3 cents per ton-kilometer. But simply having more competition on national routes would cut prices by 8 cents per ton-kilometer. For the region as a whole, allowing foreign companies to serve national routes rather than limiting them to international point-to-point trips could help bring freight costs in line with its peers (Osborne, Pachón, and Araya 2014).

Latin America ranks poorly on the World Bank's Logistics Performance Index (LPI), closer to Sub-Saharan Africa than to East Asia (figure 1.8). Disaggregating the region's overall LPI shows that this lackluster performance is due to inefficient customs clearance processes and shoddy trade and transport infrastructure. Country disparities are pronounced. Chile was the region's best performer

Figure 1.8 Latin America's 2014 Logistics Performance Index (LPI) Was Dragged Down by Poor Infrastructure Quality and Slow Customs Procedures

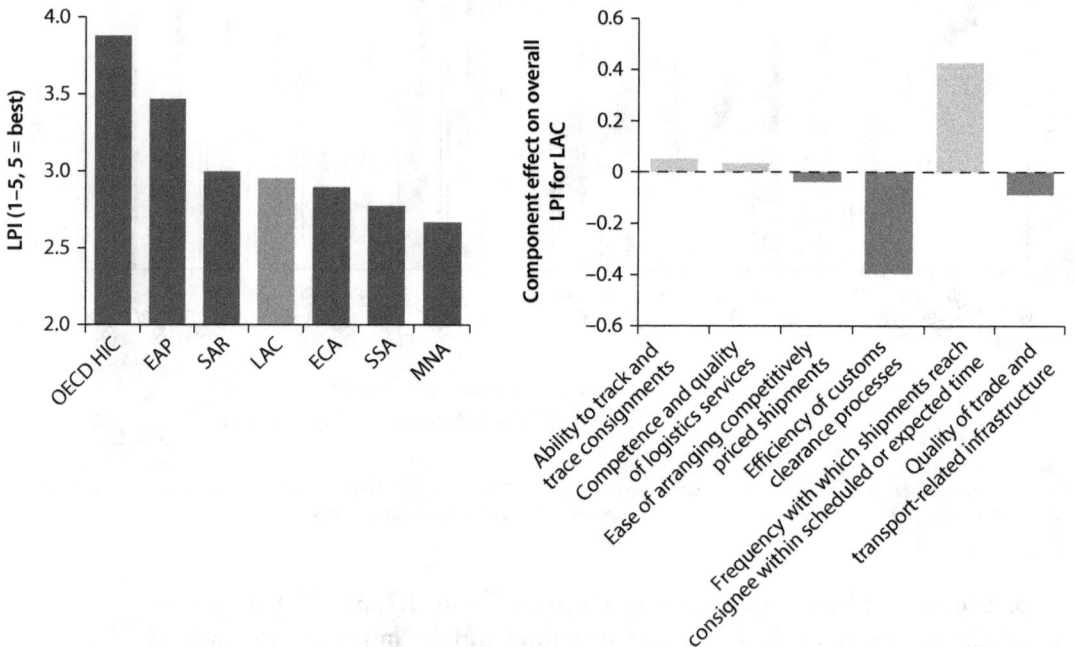

Source: http://data.worldbank.org/products/wdi.
Note: Regional averages weighted by current gross domestic product. High-income excluded from regional aggregates everywhere except the Organisation for Economic Co-operation and Development (OECD). Regions include East Asia and Pacific (EAP), South Asia (SAR), Latin America and the Caribbean (LAC), Europe and Central Asia (ECA), Sub-Saharan African (SSA), and the Middle East and North Africa (MNA), with a comparator group of high-income OECD countries (OECD HIC).

Table 1.2 Latin America's Average Export Costs and Times, Although Better than Some, Are Higher than in Competing Regions

Region	Cost to export (US$)	Time to export (hours)
Eastern Europe and Central Asia	1,133	110
Middle East and North Africa	938	253
Sub-Saharan Africa	914	257
Latin America and Caribbean	785	81
East Asia and Pacific	573	56
South Asia	542	155
OECD high-income countries	302	20

Source: World Bank 2016.
Note: OECD = Organisation for Economic Co-operation and Development. Regional averages weighted by current gross domestic product. High-income countries excluded everywhere except OECD.

in 2014, on par with the overall score for Eastern Europe and Central Asia. But Bolivia, Guatemala, Jamaica, and República Bolivariana de Venezuela were at or below the Sub-Saharan average.

The World Bank's *Doing Business* data offer a more positive diagnostic, showing Latin America to have higher costs and longer times to export than East Asia (and higher costs than South Asia), but lower costs and shorter times than other developing regions (table 1.2).

Rural Areas Are Challenged by Low Transport and Population Densities

Connecting rural communities to the "outside world" is essential for inclusive development. Good rural access can raise household welfare, asset ownership, agricultural productivity, and access to basic services. In Peru, a survey of 176 rural districts in the poorest and previously isolated areas in Andean provinces found that improved rural accessibility significantly increased agricultural wages, as well as land and housing prices, and boosted the frequency of health consultations by 70 percent (World Bank 2015).

The low density of both populations and transport infrastructure in Latin America makes it a challenge to increase rural accessibility. Further, data on rural connectivity are scarce, with few countries having geo-referenced datasets on roads that would enable the calculation of some type of rural accessibility measure (let alone some kind of rural investment optimization). A rural accessibility index estimating the share of the rural population living within 2 kilometers of an all-weather road is available for only a handful of countries in Central and South America. The index indicates that poor rural access to roads is concentrated in the Amazonian basin. But there are noticeable pockets of poor access in coastal regions of Colombia and Ecuador, and access is mixed in Honduras and Nicaragua as well (map 1.1). The need for rural access should be balanced with environmental protection, given the well-documented impact of roads on deforestation (Ali and others 2015).[5]

Map 1.1 Some Pockets of Low Road Access Overlap with Environmentally Protected Areas
Percentage of rural population living within 2 kilometers of an all-weather road

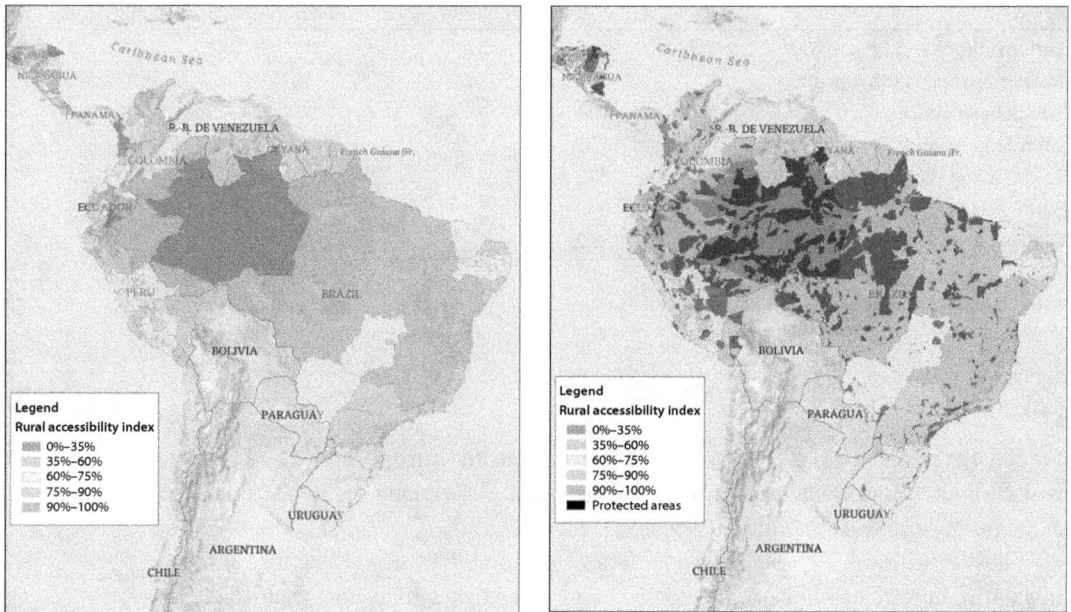

Source: World Bank estimates.

Urban Areas Suffer from Congestion and Lack of Accessibility despite the Expansion of Rapid Bus Systems

Urban areas, where 80 percent of Latin Americans live, have seen a sharp increase in the demand for and complexity of urban mobility. This is due to both population and income increases. Over the past 10 or so years, the number of people living in cities with more than 300,000 people—and so in need of reasonably sophisticated transport systems—grew by 28 percent (75 million). At the same time, income growth and a rapid expansion of the middle class have caused the number of cars and motorcycles to increase rapidly (figure 1.9): for example, from about 6 million or 7 million cars and motorcycles in 1990 in Brazil and Mexico to some 21 million or 22 million by 2010.

Rapid urbanization and increasing motorization have proven difficult for policy makers to manage. Congestion is common in many urban areas, resulting in frequent complaints about time lost in traffic. Unfortunately, limited data are available on how Latin American cities fare relative to others—data coverage only includes large Brazilian cities and Mexico City. They suggest that while congestion in the region results in long travel times for cars, it is not systematically worse than in cities elsewhere of similar size (figure 1.10). That said, striking differences between cities of similar size in the region (such as Mexico City and São Paulo) suggest that policy makers have the power to effect change.

Figure 1.9 Ownership of Two- and Four-Wheel Vehicles Spiked between 1990 and 2010

Per 1,000 people

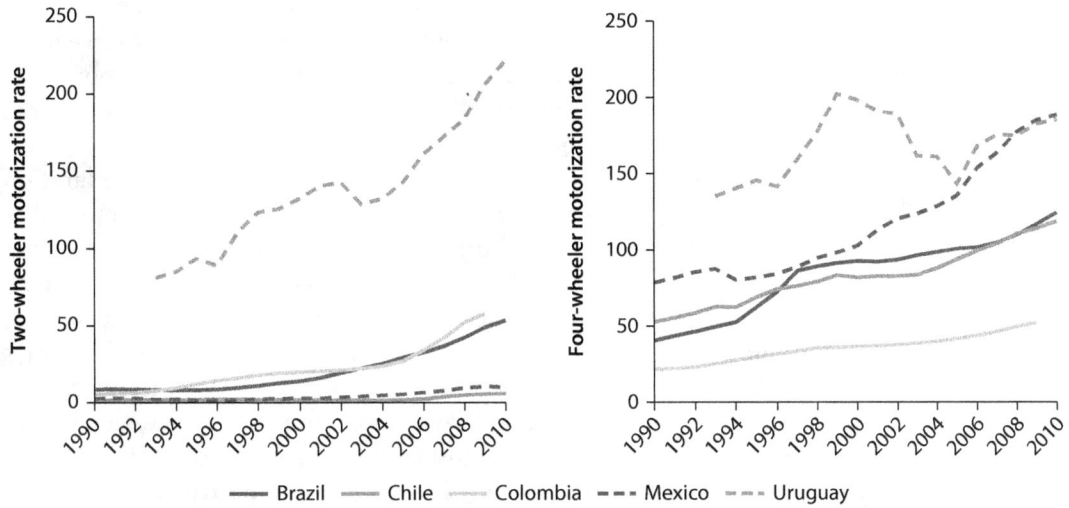

Source: ITF 2015.

Figure 1.10 Motorists' Morning Commutes Are Long in Latin America, Especially in Big Cities, but Not Necessarily Longer than in Cities Elsewhere

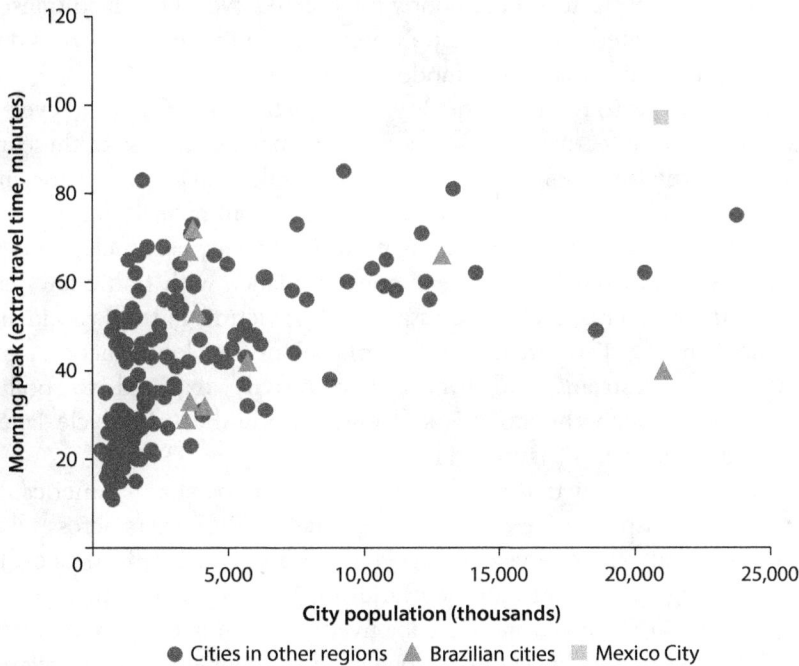

Source: Based on TomTom International 2015 and UNDESA 2014.
Note: Extra travel time defined as percentage additional time needed relative to free-flowing traffic. Red triangles are Brazilian cities, the green square is Mexico City, and blue dots represent cities outside Latin America.

The past decade has seen significant investments in large-scale public transport systems in key Latin American cities where population densities justify the investments. Many urban centers now have multiple public transport modes. Bus rapid transit (BRT) systems have grown rapidly in the region and now serve more than 20 million passengers a day. Among Latin American cities with more than 1 million inhabitants, 59 percent have BRT systems, 31 percent have urban rail systems, and 25 percent have both.[6]

Some BRTs have become victims of their own success, as there is a limit on the number of passengers they can serve each day. When ridership approaches 700,000–800,000 passengers a day, urban transport systems have to consider diversifying—especially if urban planning or physical geography do not allow BRT systems to expand. That was the case in Quito, Ecuador, which is now planning its first underground rail mass transit system. Metro systems and subways have become increasingly viable modes of transport in large cities with high population densities. Where urban rail systems are already in place, the density of service per resident remains low in most countries. Except for Santiago, Chile, Latin American cities have substantially less urban rail infrastructure than their counterparts in OECD countries.

Non–mass transit systems remain poor, also challenged by the region's rapid urbanization. City blocks are often infilled, leaving no space for pavement. This creates problems for pedestrians, who might be forced to walk in traffic, making walking dangerous during the day and almost impossible at night. And where pavement exists, it is often poorly maintained. Nonmotorized transport is seldom well-integrated with public transportation and is too often considered a peripheral issue rather than a key mode of transport.

As part of efforts to reduce inequality, high-quality pavements and cycle lanes are extremely cost effective because poor people make heavy use of these investments. They are also essential in providing last-mile transportation for citizens who need to reach mass transit such as BRTs and urban rail systems quickly and safely. Inadequate infrastructure for nonmotorized transport (such as sidewalks and dedicated bike lanes) and drivers' noncompliance with traffic laws expose users to traffic accidents, thefts, and assaults. Most victims in traffic accidents are pedestrians and cyclists, many of whom belong to lower-income groups. In addition, pedestrians and cyclists are heavily exposed to pollution. Encouragingly, though the stock is still low, the number of bicycle lanes has exploded in recent years (figure 1.11).

The quality of urban transport remains mixed across Latin America. Some newer public transport systems are of high quality. BRT users across all Latin America cities rate their service a respectable 3.5 out of 5 (BRTdata.org). The cost of an average mass transit journey varies substantially across the region, with the average fare in São Paulo and Curitiba five times that in Quito and Guayaquil (figure 1.12). Whether this is due to longer transit, higher costs, or greater cost recovery in the tariffs is unclear.

Figure 1.11 Although Their Number Is Low, Bicycle Lanes Are Expanding in Latin America, 2011

Kilometers of bicycle lanes per million urban inhabitants

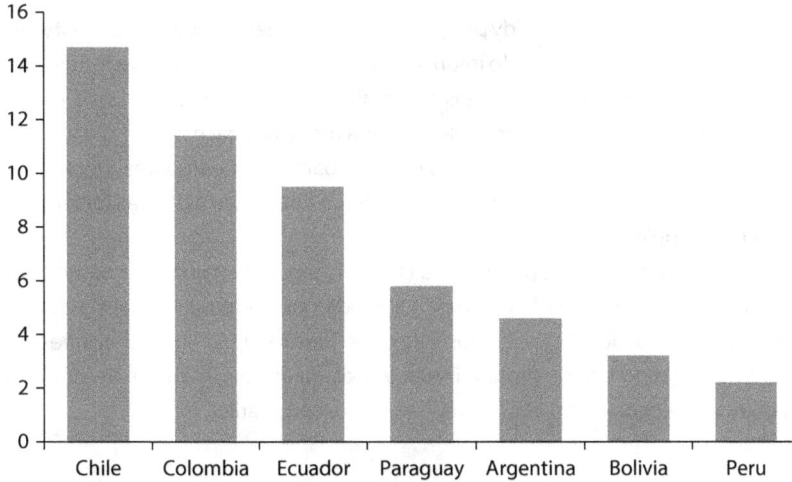

Source: Hidalgo 2011.

Figure 1.12 The Average Mass Transit Journey Costs More in Latin America than in Many Other Places, 2009
U.S. dollars

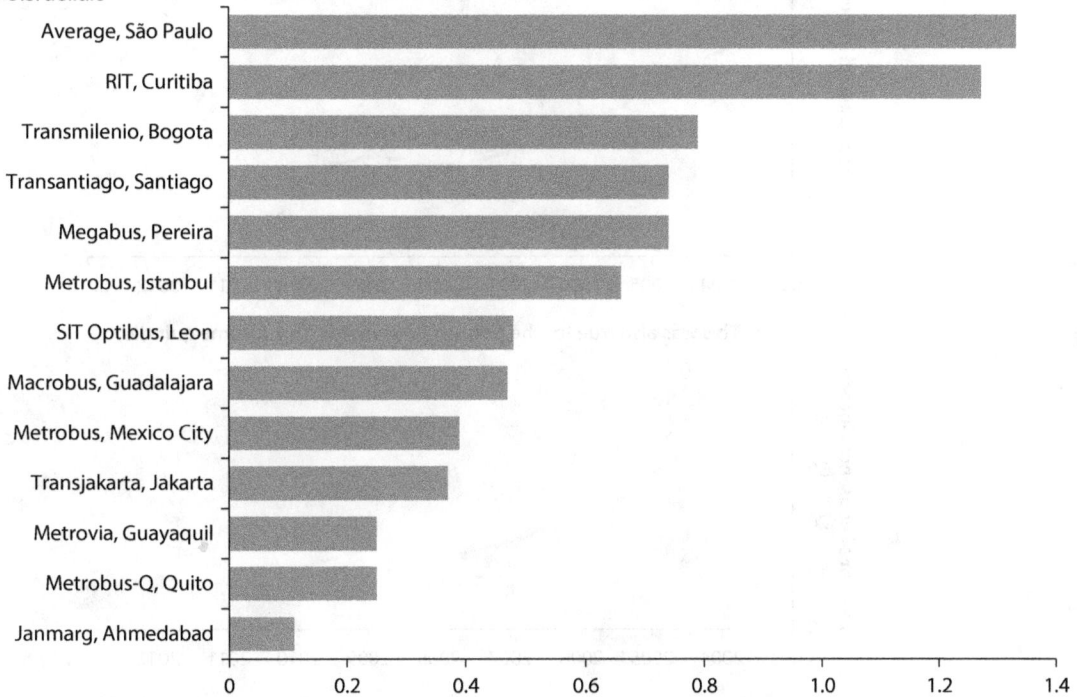

Source: Cubas and others 2015.
Note: RIT = Rede Integrada de Transporte de Curitiba; SIT = Sistema Integrado de Transporte.

Box 1.2 Using a Fare Affordability Index to Guide a Subsidy Program in Buenos Aires

While the scale and scope of a subsidy program are political decisions based on a city's finances and other goals, certain tools can help inform choices on who should receive funding and how much they should receive. An example is a fare affordability index to measure the financial impact of a standard basket of transit trips—say, 45 a month for each household member—on various income groups. Figure B1.2.1 shows this approach for Buenos Aires, where the afford-ability of public transport was measured for an average household as well as for families in the lowest income quintile.

Affordability depends on the alternatives (say, walking and cycling) and other costs of liv-ing, including housing. Still, the fare affordability index can help policy makers as they think about different subsidy levels. In Buenos Aires, the index helped show that fares could be raised considerably and still be more affordable—as measured by the share of income the poorest quintile spent on a basket of travel—than a decade earlier.

Figure B1.2.1 Affordability of Public Transport in Buenos Aires, 2003–13

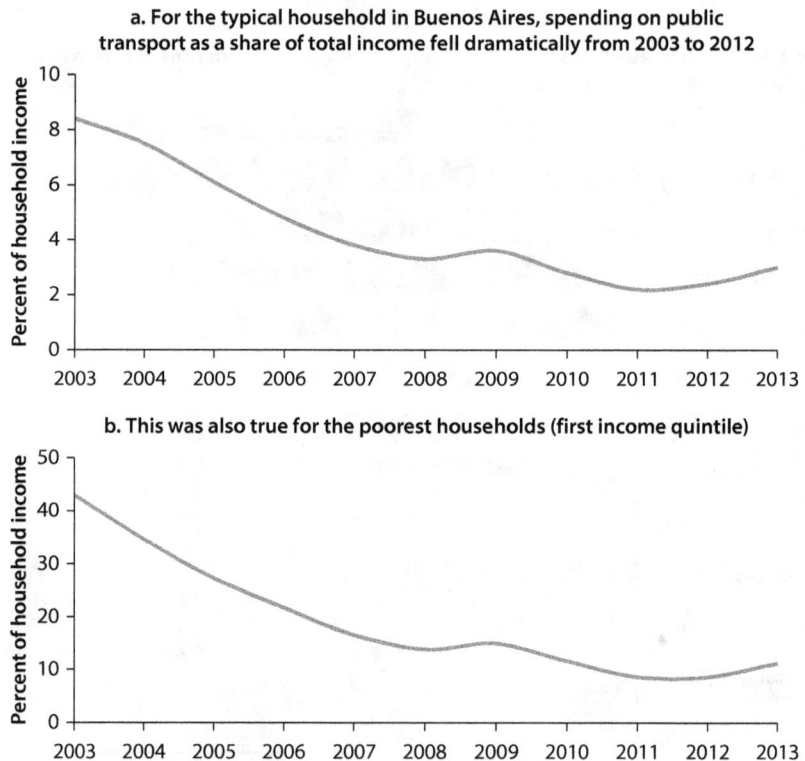

a. For the typical household in Buenos Aires, spending on public transport as a share of total income fell dramatically from 2003 to 2012

b. This was also true for the poorest households (first income quintile)

Source: Mehndiratta, Rodriguez, and Ochoa 2014.

Without targeted demand-side subsidies, public transport can be unaffordable for low-income groups. Household surveys from Bogota, Buenos Aires, Santo Domingo, and São Paulo found that commuting on the formal public transport system could eat up 20–30 percent of poor households' budgets (Cubas and others 2015). And although there is not an accepted ceiling for what households should spend on transport, a fare affordability index can help guide policy decisions on existing or potential subsidies (box 1.2).

Latin American countries have struggled to devise affordable, effective subsidies for public transport. One common approach is to set fares for cost recovery but offer targeted demand-side subsidies for specific population groups (Gwilliams 2012; Mehndiratta, Rodriguez, and Ochoa 2014; Serebrisky and others 2009). But experience with demand-side subsidies is mixed, with difficulties identifying and reaching target populations and potential abuse of subsidies (such as transferring them to unintended recipients). Other approaches have included Bilete Unico, operational in Rio de Janeiro and São Paulo, which caps the fare for multimodal trips and subsidizes feeder transport (such as cable cars in Rio de Janeiro and Medellín that connect poorer neighborhoods to main transit arteries and allow a certain number of free trips per day [Rodriguez and others 2016]). But both programs contribute to urban sprawl and suffer from errors of inclusion (wealthier persons using these lower-cost options).

Encouragingly, subsidy efforts are becoming more sophisticated as technology makes disbursement more effective and efficient. In Bogota, transport subsidies are disbursed on travel cards linked to the Sistema Nacional de Selección de Beneficiarios (SISBEN), the national database of potential beneficiaries for social support programs (TransMilenio 2015, Rodriguez and others 2016). The program disburses the subsidy as a half-off fare when the card is used to pay for public transport (capped at 40 trips a month). The program builds on the growing use of electronic fare media (smart cards) in Bogotá's public transit systems and national experience with other poverty-targeting initiatives (such as conditional cash transfer programs) that use SISBEN. Fraud attempts are deterred through the use of biometric identification and requirements for photo IDs.

Still, the continued strong presence of informal transport modes indicates that transport needs are not being met by formal public transport services. Informal transport systems are especially common among poorer households that are not served by or cannot afford formal transport. Relative to formal transport, informal transport can be more accessible, flexible, reliable, faster, and cheaper. But the vehicles are typically not suited to collective transport. They are often unregulated, in oversupply, unsafe, and unpredictable. And even though informal transport is an important source of employment, it is also a major cause of congestion and pollution. The most common examples of informal transport systems are the vans and mini/micro buses used in cities like Brasilia, San Salvador, and Santo Domingo. Other examples are motorcycle taxis in Lima, Fortaleza, and Santo Domingo (Jirón 2013).

More generally, safety is a major challenge, with traffic deaths a serious issue across Latin America, and not just in urban areas. When weighted by population, the death rate from road traffic accidents in the region is more than 19 per 100,000 people—three to four times that in Europe (UN-Habitat 2013). In addition, women are often sexually harassed on public transport, undermining their ability to safely participate in economic and social activities (box 1.3).

Water and Sanitation: Good Coverage for Water, but Sanitation an Increasingly Urgent Challenge

Good water and sanitation coverage is critical to public health, especially in areas with high human density, pollution, or both. In addition, inadequate access usually implies that households have to spend more time and money getting water. While Latin America has made good progress on increasing the share of households with access to water, it has not done as well on sanitation. Many households lack access to improved sanitation, and only about 30 percent of the region's wastewater is treated. These shortfalls caused a loss of 941,000 disability-adjusted life years (DALYs) across the region in 2012, concentrated in Bolivia, Brazil, Guatemala, Haiti, and Mexico (figure 1.13).

Water and sanitation have traditionally represented a small share of Latin America's investments in infrastructure, hovering between a quarter and a third of a percent of GDP (figure 1.14). Funding has predominantly come from the public sector, though the past few years have seen an increase in private funding that has helped offset a dip in public spending.

Water: Good Progress on Access, but No Room for Complacency

Some 94 percent of households have access to an improved source of drinking water, placing Latin America in the top ranks of developing regions—though still short of the 99 percent in high-income countries (figure 1.15, panel a).

Box 1.3 Public Transport for All? Sexual Harassment Is a Major Issue on Public Transport in Latin America

Safety for women is one component of transport quality that is often overlooked. Sexual harassment and assault are higher in Latin America's major metropolitan areas than elsewhere. Women in the region consistently report feeling less safe than women in European metropolitan areas. In Bogotá, Lima, Mexico City, and Santiago, 60–90 percent of women report experiencing sexual harassment or assault on public transport in any given year. Actual levels of sexual harassment and assault could be higher because reporting rates are low. Brazil and Mexico have implemented "women-only" cars on trains and subways. But their reception has been mixed; some argue that they do not address the cultural norms that reinforce sexual violence, while others note that they pose issues for women traveling with boys or elderly men.

Sources: Balbotín and Arredondo 2015; Jaimurzina, Salas, and Sánchez 2015.

Figure 1.13 Inadequate Water and Sanitation Impose a Health Burden in Latin America, 2012

DALYs lost because of inadequate water and sanitation

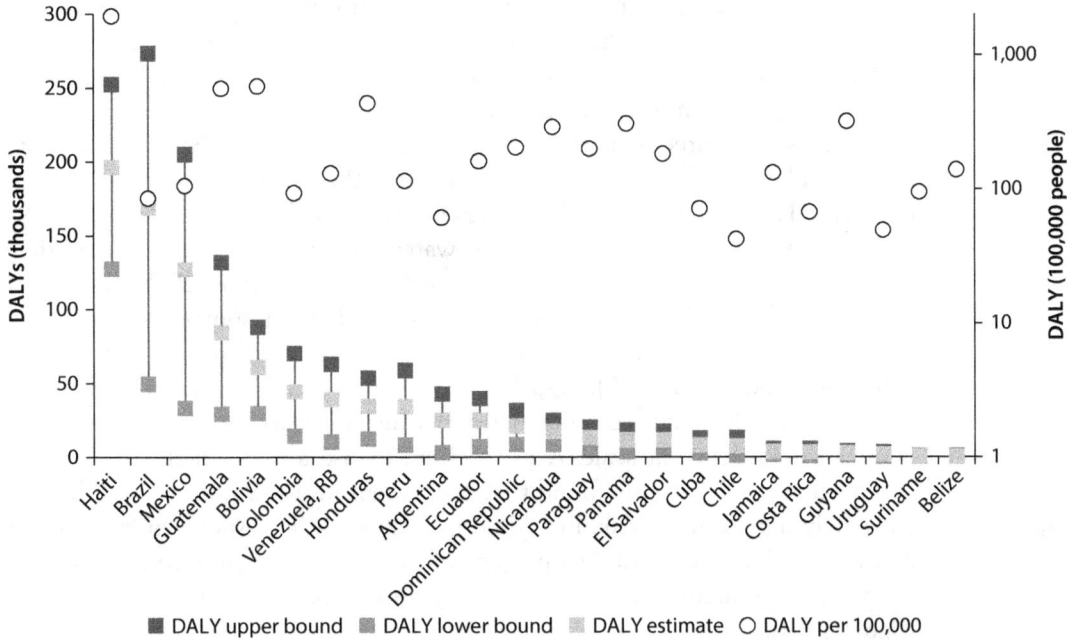

DALY upper bound   ■ DALY lower bound   ■ DALY estimate   ○ DALY per 100,000

Source: WHO and UNICEF 2016.
Note: One DALY can be thought of as one year of healthy life. The sum of DALYs lost across a population can be thought of as a measure of the gap between current health status and an ideal health situation where the entire population lives to an advanced age, free of disease and disability. DALY = disability-adjusted life year.

Figure 1.14 Water and Sanitation Investments in Latin America Were Modest in 2000–12

Percentage of GDP

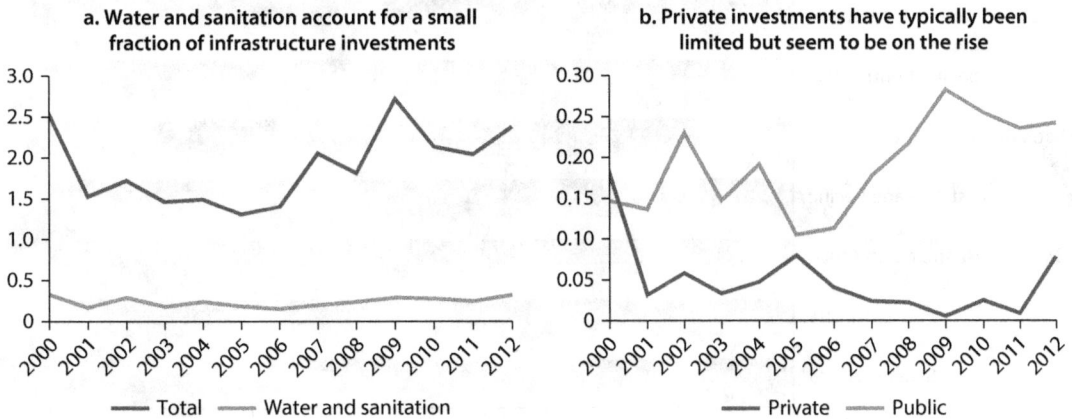

a. Water and sanitation account for a small fraction of infrastructure investments

— Total   — Water and sanitation

b. Private investments have typically been limited but seem to be on the rise

— Private   — Public

Source: http://www.infralatam.info, downloaded November 15, 2016.
Note: GDP = gross domestic product.

Moreover, this average masks a large gap between rural (84 percent) and urban (97 percent) coverage (figure 1.15, panel b). In fact, whereas coverage is lower for poor households, the rural/urban divide trumps income as a marker for lack of access to an improved drinking water source (figure 1.15, panel c).

The region's relatively high coverage is no cause for complacency. More than 20 million people, mostly in rural areas, lack access to an improved source of drinking water, three-quarters of them in six countries—Brazil, Colombia, Ecuador, Haiti, Mexico, and Peru—that include the region's richest and poorest countries. The type of service also differs between rural and urban areas, with 94 of the urban population with access to water served with piped water on their premises, but only 68 percent in rural areas (WHO and UNICEF 2016).

Further, the quality of "access to an improved water source" is often poor. About a quarter of those with access get it by informal means (Borja-Vega, Perochena, and Zuilu 2015).[7] Quality is often inadequate, with implications for public health. But data are weak, partly because measuring water quality is difficult and expensive at scale. A pilot effort to use a rapid quality assessment deployed across Nicaragua found that 16 percent of water points posed high to extremely high sanitary risk. In addition, reliability is an issue even in relatively privileged urban areas, with 13 percent of the population surveyed in a sample of the region's largest cities reporting they do not have continuous daily service (figure 1.16).

Figure 1.15 Impressive Progress on Access to Water, although Rural and Poor Populations Still Less Likely to Be Served

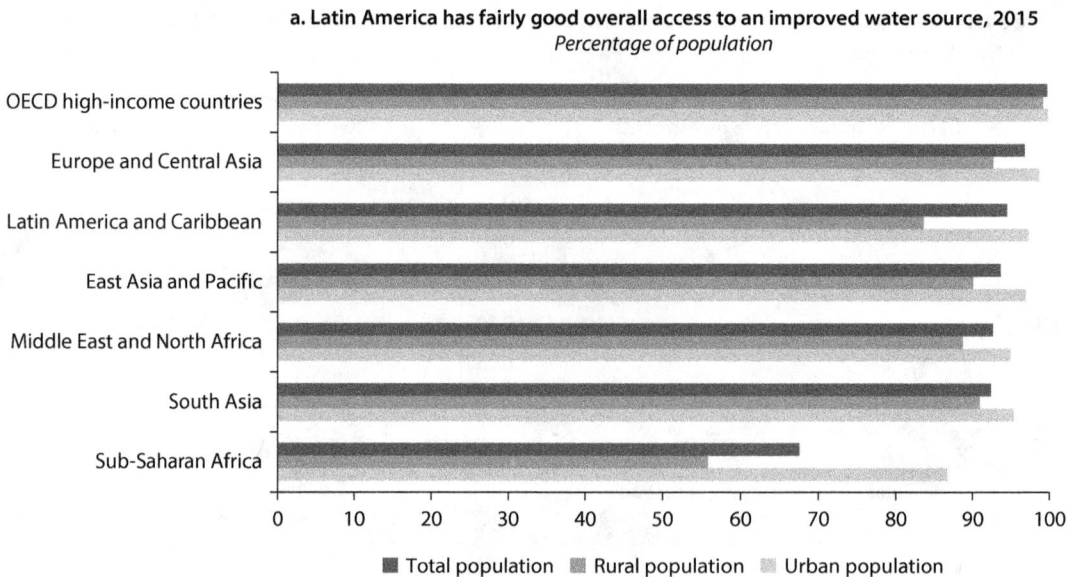

a. Latin America has fairly good overall access to an improved water source, 2015
Percentage of population

Note: OECD = Organisation for Economic Co-operation and Development. The Republic of Korea excluded from OECD high-income countries because of a lack of data.

figure continues next page

Figure 1.15 Impressive Progress on Access to Water, although Rural and Poor Populations Still Less Likely to be Served *(continued)*

b. But with wide variation across the region, especially among rural populations
Percentage of population

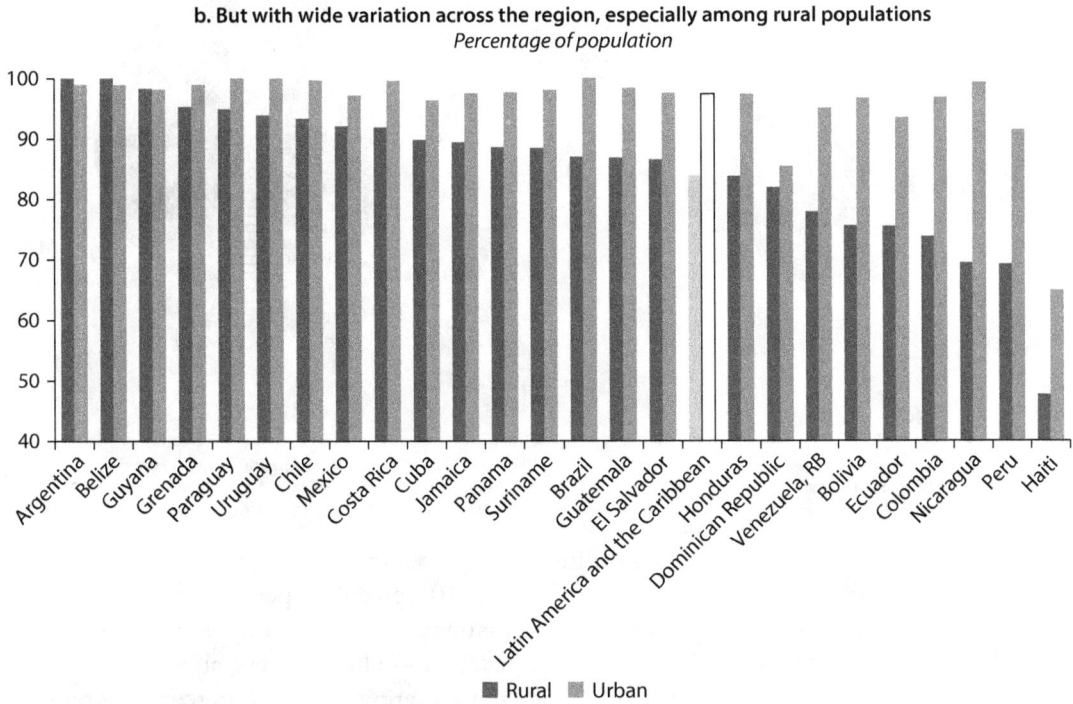

Rural ▮ Urban ▮

c. Wealth matters for water access, especially in rural areas, 2012
Percentage of population with access to an improved water source, by rural and urban wealth quintile

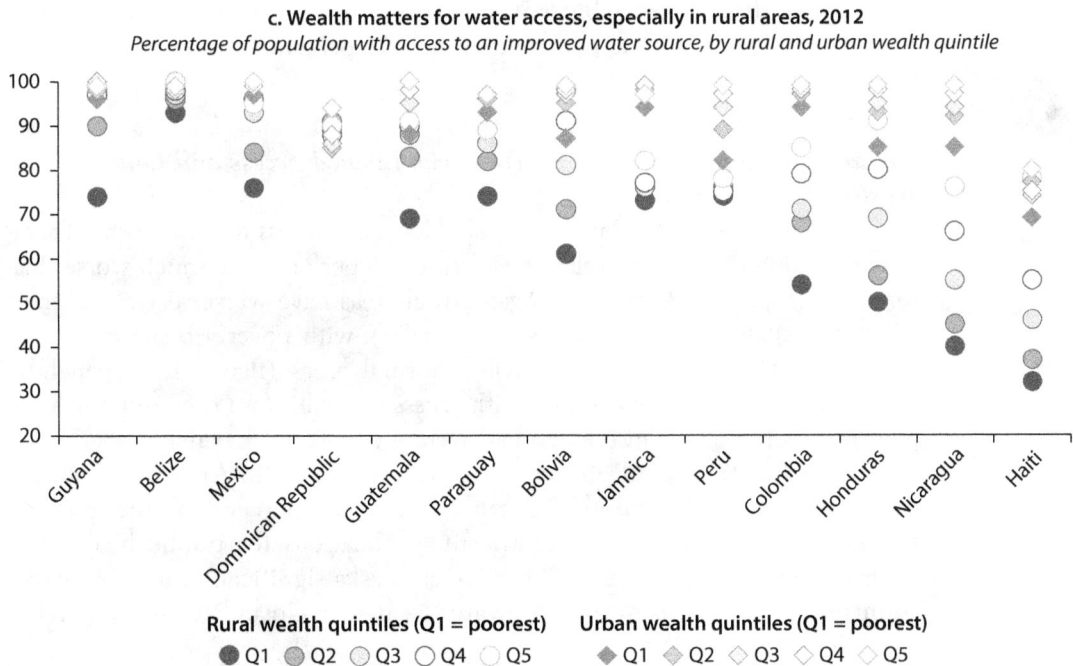

Rural wealth quintiles (Q1 = poorest)
● Q1 ● Q2 ◐ Q3 ○ Q4 ○ Q5

Urban wealth quintiles (Q1 = poorest)
◆ Q1 ◆ Q2 ◇ Q3 ◇ Q4 ◇ Q5

Source: WHO and UNICEF 2016.

Figure 1.16 Reliability of Water Service Is an Issue for Many, 2008–13
Percentage of households

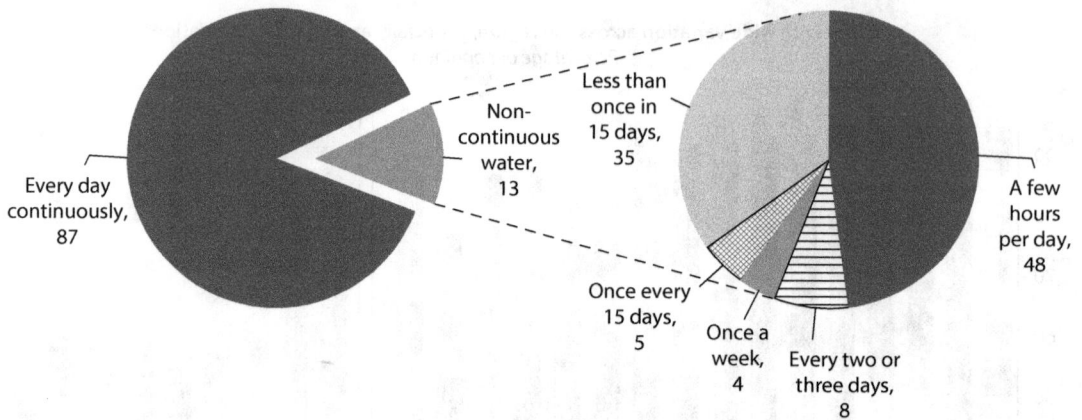

Every day continuously, 87

Non-continuous water, 13

Less than once in 15 days, 35

A few hours per day, 48

Once every 15 days, 5

Once a week, 4

Every two or three days, 8

Source: CAF 2014, based on a survey conducted in Argentina (Buenos Aires, Córdoba, Rafaela), Bolivia (Cochabamba, La Paz, Santa Cruz), Brazil (Nueva Iguazu, Rio de Janeiro, San Pablo), Colombia (Barranquilla, Bogotá, Medellín), Ecuador (Manta, Quito, Guayaquil), Peru (Arequito, Peru, Piura), Uruguay (Montevideo, Salto), República Bolivariana de Venezuela (Caracas, Maracaibo, San Cristóbal), Panama (Panama City), and Mexico (Mexico City).

While Latin America's utilities perform reasonably well, most could do better, as measured by their gap with the top 10 percent of performers (figure 1.17). The middle 80 percent in the International Benchmarking Network for Water and Sanitation Utilities (IBNET) database—which covers about 1,900 Latin American utilities—average 80 percent metering, about 30 percent nonrevenue water (that is, water lost or stolen, for which the utilities do not charge), and can cover operational expenses but not much more from revenues. In contrast, the top 10 percent achieve 100 percent metering, 15 percent nonrevenue water, and full cost recovery.

Sanitation Performance Remains Poor, with Limited Access and Low Wastewater Treatment

Only 83 percent of Latin America's population has access to some form of sanitation, making the region's relative and absolute performance much worse than for water (figure 1.18, panel a). Again, rural areas have worse service coverage (64 percent) than do urban areas (88 percent), with poverty being more of a marker for lack of access than living in rural areas (figure 1.18, panel b). Colombia and Paraguay stand out, with access in the bottom rural quintile at 40 percent—half or less than the national average (figure 1.18, panel c).

Wastewater treatment and reuse is also low in Latin America. Data are scarce, but it is estimated that only about 30 percent of the region's wastewater is treated—with significant implications for public health and environmental sustainability. This average masks significant variation across countries, from 4 percent of wastewater treated in Costa Rica to 99 percent in Chile (figure 1.19).

Figure 1.17 Most Latin American Utilities Perform Reasonably Well but Could Do Better, as Illustrated by the Top Performers

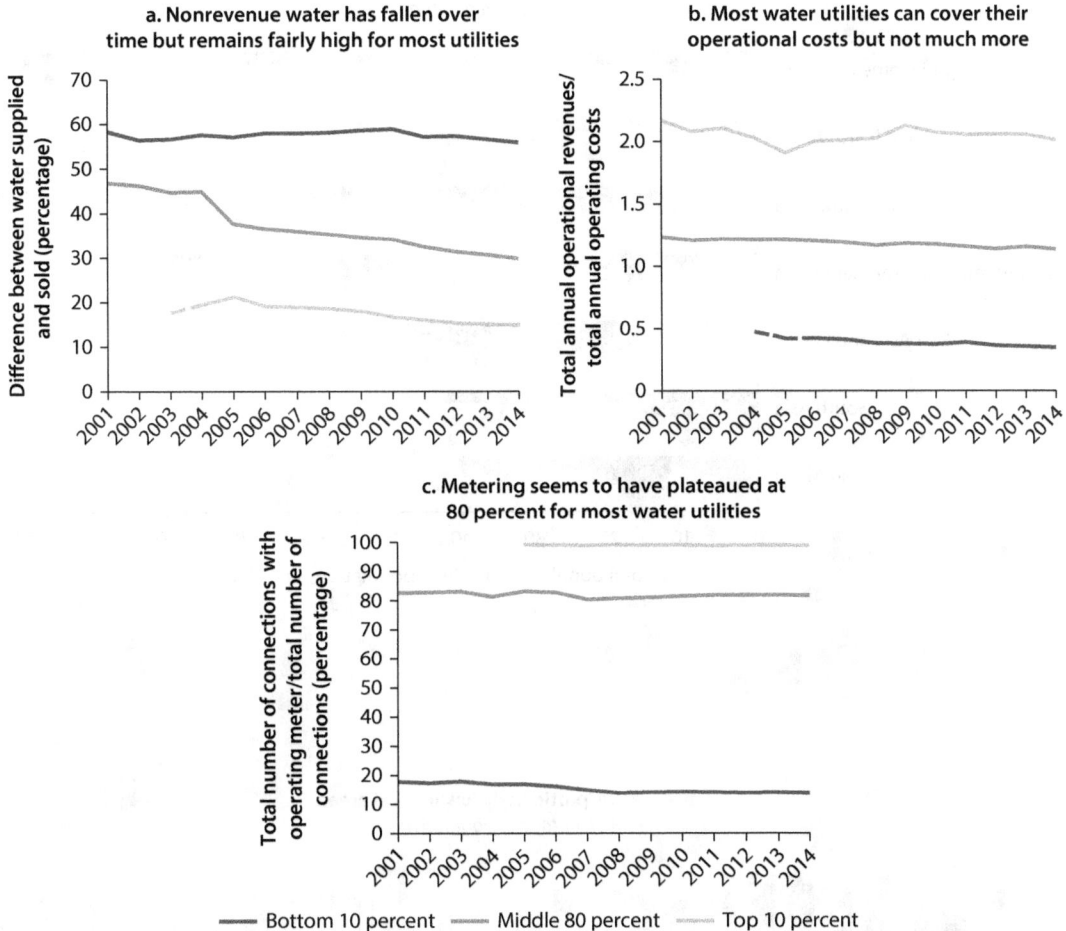

a. Nonrevenue water has fallen over time but remains fairly high for most utilities

b. Most water utilities can cover their operational costs but not much more

c. Metering seems to have plateaued at 80 percent for most water utilities

— Bottom 10 percent — Middle 80 percent — Top 10 percent

Source: Analysis courtesy of Luis Andrès and Aroha Bahuguna using IBNET data. Dashed lines indicate fewer than 10 but more than 5 observations. The solid lines indicate more than 10 observations.

One of the most concerning aspects of the institutional environment for wastewater is the inadequate attention paid to the regulating, monitoring, and enforcing provisions designed to restrict industrial discharge into receiving water bodies. Enforcement of industrial pretreatment to remove heavy metals, organic compounds, and other contaminants is needed to prevent damage to pipe infrastructure, ensure that biological treatment processes work effectively, and keep harmful concentrations from preventing the reuse of sludge as a fertilizer.

The poor performance of most Latin American countries in wastewater treatment stands out compared to other infrastructure sectors, and so merits more

Figure 1.18 Latin America Has Not Done as Well on Providing Access to Improved Sanitation

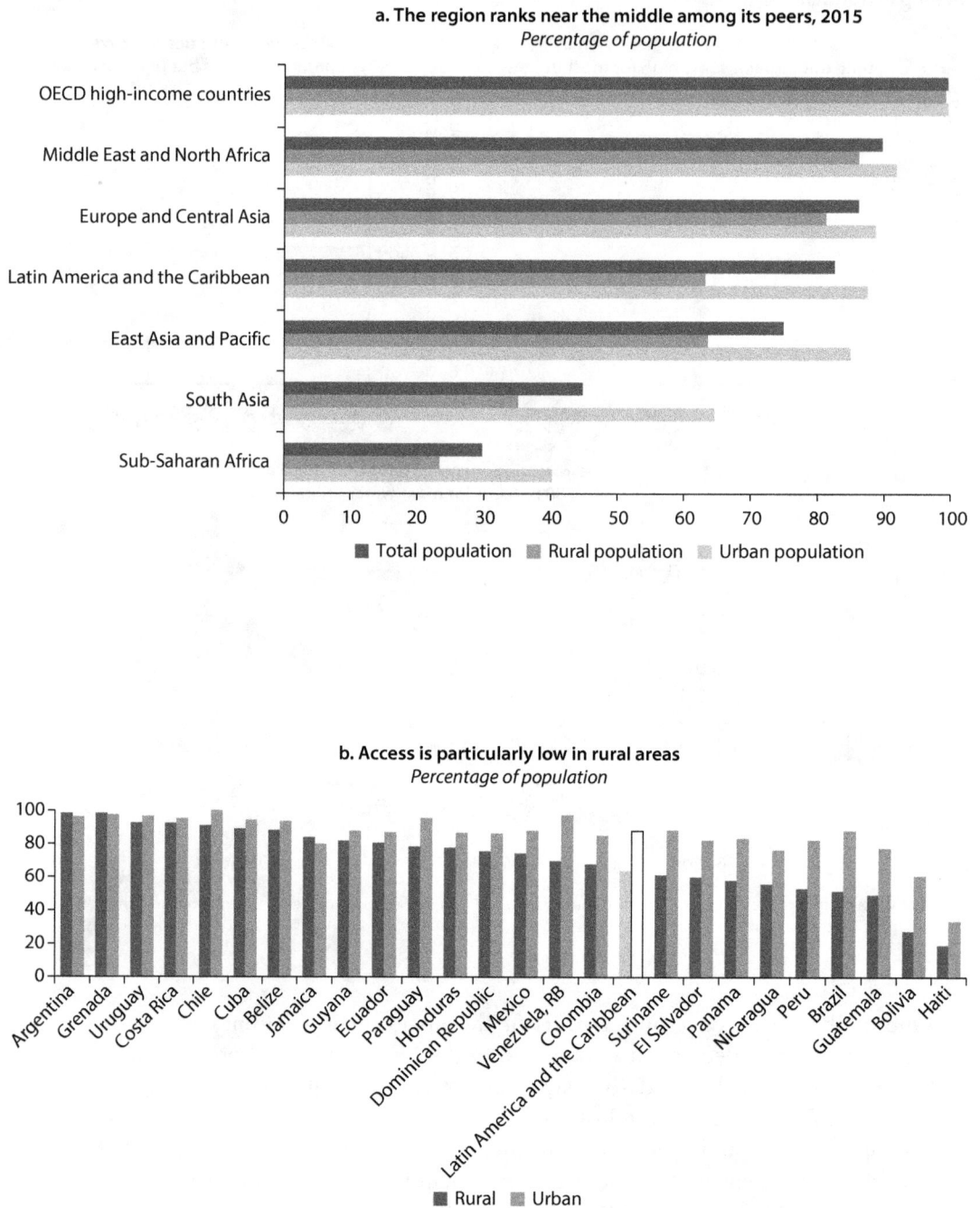

a. The region ranks near the middle among its peers, 2015
Percentage of population

Legend: ■ Total population ■ Rural population ■ Urban population

b. Access is particularly low in rural areas
Percentage of population

Legend: ■ Rural ■ Urban

figure continues next page

Figure 1.18 Latin America Has Not Done as Well on Providing Access to Improved Sanitation *(continued)*

c. Sanitation coverage is much lower among the poor, especially in rural areas, 2012
Percentage of population with access to improved sanitation by rural and urban wealth quintile

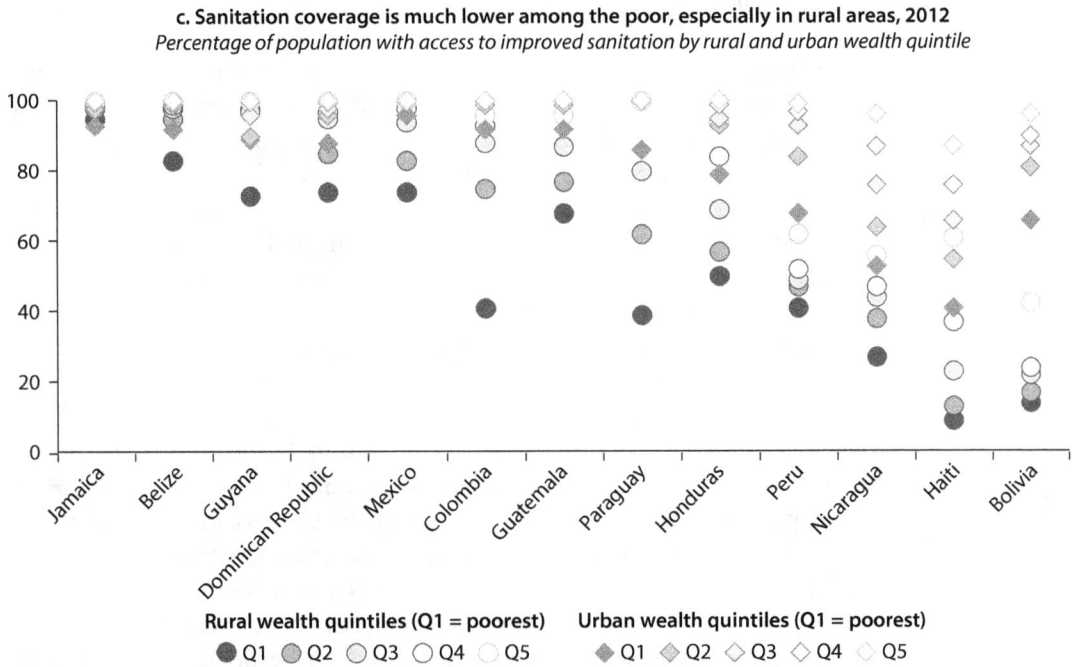

Rural wealth quintiles (Q1 = poorest)   ● Q1 ● Q2 ○ Q3 ○ Q4 ○ Q5

Urban wealth quintiles (Q1 = poorest)   ◆ Q1 ◈ Q2 ◇ Q3 ◇ Q4 ◇ Q5

Source: WHO and UNICEF 2016.
Note: OECD = Organisation for Economic Co-operation and Development. New Zealand excluded from OECD high-income countries because of lack of data.

Figure 1.19 On Average, about a Third of Wastewater in Latin America Is Treated
Percentage of wastewater treated

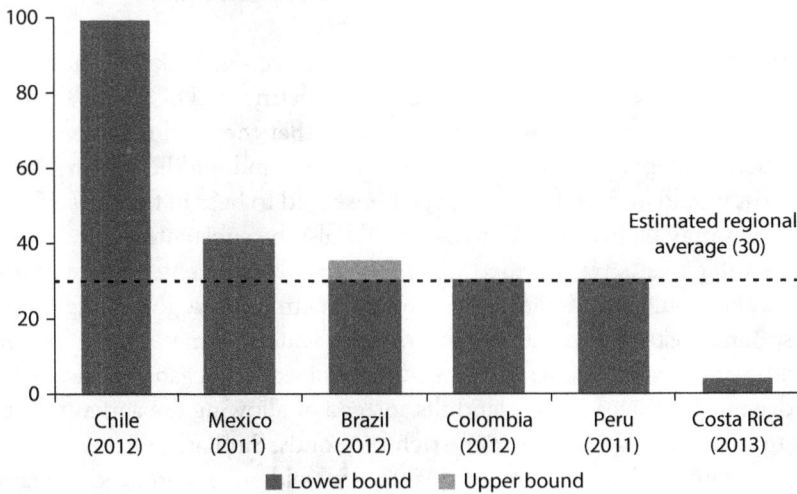

■ Lower bound ■ Upper bound

Source: Nolasco 2016.

in-depth analysis. Background work for this report identifies several causes of this poor performance (Nolasco 2016):

- *Split responsibilities between central government agencies that fund construction and local governments without the technical and financial resources to run treatment plants.* In Mexico, for example, the federal government is responsible for designing and constructing wastewater treatment plants, while cities are charged with their operation and maintenance. But most cities do not charge for sanitation. Where costs are passed on to users, tariffs are often insufficient to cover even operating costs. This disconnect between the central agency that designs and builds wastewater treatment facilities and the subnational agencies that operate them also exists in Argentina and Peru.

- *Overly ambitious "imported" regulations that leave no room for gradualism.* Many Latin American countries have adopted legislation developed in high-income countries that have strong institutional and technical capacity and high financial support from both government and users. Such legislation often imposes standards that are unrealistic and unaffordable. To illustrate: in Cordoba, Argentina, legislation implemented in 2015 requires that wastewater being discharged has a level of cleanliness that few treatment plants can meet even in high-income countries. The cost of operating the Cordoba plant far exceeds the municipality's financing capacity. Further, in most countries, regulation is binding from the day of its passage, instead of offering a path toward gradual improvement in treatment coverage and quality. The region would be better served by focusing on a progressive array of appropriate treatment technologies, starting with cheaper, lower-cost solutions, followed by upgrades to more advanced technologies as and when financial resources allow.

- *Limitations on resource recovery.* Few utilities, even in high-income countries, charge users the full cost of wastewater treatment. This is partly because households are reluctant to pay for a service that they feel may benefit others as much as themselves, but also because in low- and middle-income countries the cost would be high for an average household to bear in full. As such, public subsidies may be justified. But costs could also be substantially lowered—and wastewater plants transformed from cost to revenue centers—if countries in the region could stop treating wastewater treatment sludge as dangerous solid waste and instead allow the reuse of gray waters. Lima, a large city in the middle of a desert, discharges its wastewater into the ocean and disposes of its sludge in expensive sanitary landfills, instead of allowing the agriculture industry to make use of these nutrient-rich bio solids. Similarly, efforts to use electricity generated by treatment plants are seldom encouraged. Exceptions include the Tenorio treatment plant in San Luis Potosi, Mexico, which provides advanced primary treatment for 60 percent of the wastewater (which is then used for irrigation), and generates electricity for both own consumption and for sale—saving US$18 million over a six-year period.

- *Infrastructure not adapted for poor people.* Sewerage systems often suffer if they provide piping through neighborhoods, because either resources or interest is lacking to make final connections between the piping and businesses. Examples abound. In Guayaquil, Ecuador, where 30,000 households remain unconnected 30 years after sewerage pipes were installed, about 31 percent of households surveyed noted that money was a key impediment to connection (Poveda and others 2014). A number of countries in the region have developed schemes to tackle this issue (box 1.4).

Energy: A Sector at a Turning Point?

Latin America's energy sector could be at a turning point (World Bank, forthcoming a). The region is well positioned to close the remaining access gap—at least for electricity, as the need for clean and efficient cooking fuel has not received enough support in most countries. But shifts in demand associated with urbanization and a growing middle class, together with climate change, are creating both new challenges and opportunities.

Box 1.4 Innovative Schemes to Expand Sewerage Services across Latin America

In Brazil, where cost is a significant barrier to the expansion of sewerage in major cities, at least three utilities have taken steps to create more pro-poor services. EMBASA, Bahia state's utility, implemented an innovative program between 1995 and 2007 to introduce "condominial" sewerage to low-income neighborhoods. This program was a city block-based approach that relied on community consultations to design low-cost joint sewerage facilities. It placed the responsibility for final linkups on groups of households rather than individual households.

Similar schemes have been pioneered by CAESB, Brasilia's state water utility. Under its condominial scheme, connections to the main public sewers are constructed after the targeted community signs an agreement setting out the rights and obligations of all partners. The investment cost of the system is kept low by the use of small bore pipes, starting at diameters of just 100 millimeters (Shankland and others 2010). Another Brazilian utility, SABESP, targeted the last-mile problem by offering subsidies and payment by installment for connecting households to sewerage services. Finally, in the state of Minas Gerais, the state water utility COPASA has established a subsidiary that offers pro-poor tariffication and technologies. Colombia, Peru, and Uruguay are also implementing projects to tackle sewerage for the poor, but those countries have yet to develop them at scale.

Elsewhere, public-private partnerships for wastewater treatment plants appear to be working well. A perfect example is the Atotonilco de Tula plant in Mexico, which treats wastewater generated in the valley of Mexico. It is 54 percent funded by the private sector and is operated by a private consortium. There are also examples of private businesses building wastewater treatment plants to make use of municipally discharged wastewater—for example, the Enlozada-Cerro Verde treatment plant in Arequipa, Peru, was built and operated by the mining company Cerro Verde, which uses the treated water at its mine site.

Source: Nolasco 2016.

Figure 1.20 Energy Investments in Latin America Are Rebounding, 2000–12

Percentage of GDP

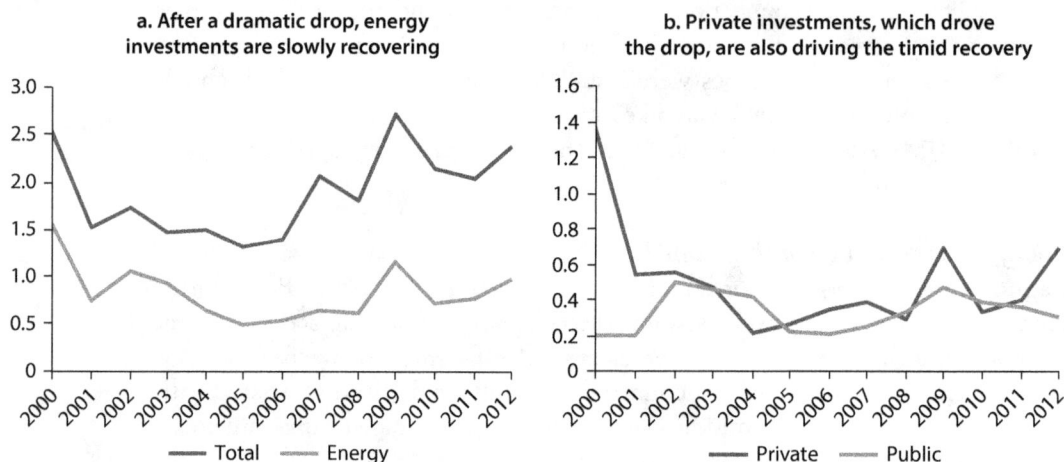

a. After a dramatic drop, energy investments are slowly recovering

b. Private investments, which drove the drop, are also driving the timid recovery

— Total   — Energy

— Private   — Public

Source: http://www.infralatam.info, downloaded November 15, 2016.
Note: GDP = gross domestic product.

Investments in energy dropped dramatically in the early 2000s and have been slowly recovering since, hovering around 0.75–1.00 percent of GDP in recent years (figure 1.20, panel a). The drop was driven by a sharp and sudden decline in private flows to the sector, from about 1.4 percent of GDP in 2000 to about 0.2 percent four years later. Private flows have slowly and unevenly increased in recent years, to account for some two-thirds of energy investments in the region in 2012 (figure 1.20, panel b).

If Given Enough Attention, the Access Gap Could Be Closed

Latin America has fairly high access to electricity and modern (nonsolid) fuels, with access rates of 96 percent in electricity and 84 percent in nonsolid fuels (figure 1.21). This is well above the developing country averages, estimated at 86 percent and 59 percent, and on par with the middle-income average for electricity.

Nevertheless, 22 million Latin Americans remain without access to electricity (more than half of them in Haiti and rural Guatemala and Peru), and 87 million lack access to nonsolid fuels (three-quarters of them in Brazil, Guatemala, Haiti, Mexico, and Peru; figure 1.22). Electrification rates are increasing throughout the region, but for access to nonsolid fuels, slow progress in a number of countries (such as Guatemala and República Bolivariana de Venezuela) means that these countries are unlikely to attain universal access any time soon.

A major issue is inequality of access for both electricity and nonsolid fuels—not only in countries with lower levels of access such as Haiti, Guatemala, Guyana, and Honduras, but also in upper-middle-income countries such as Brazil, Chile, and Mexico. Access is mostly a challenge in rural areas, but some periurban areas and slums lack access or have unreliable, illegal, and unsafe

Figure 1.21 Access to Electricity and Nonsolid Fuels Is High, but Not Relative to Peers and Not in Rural Areas, 2012
Percentage of population

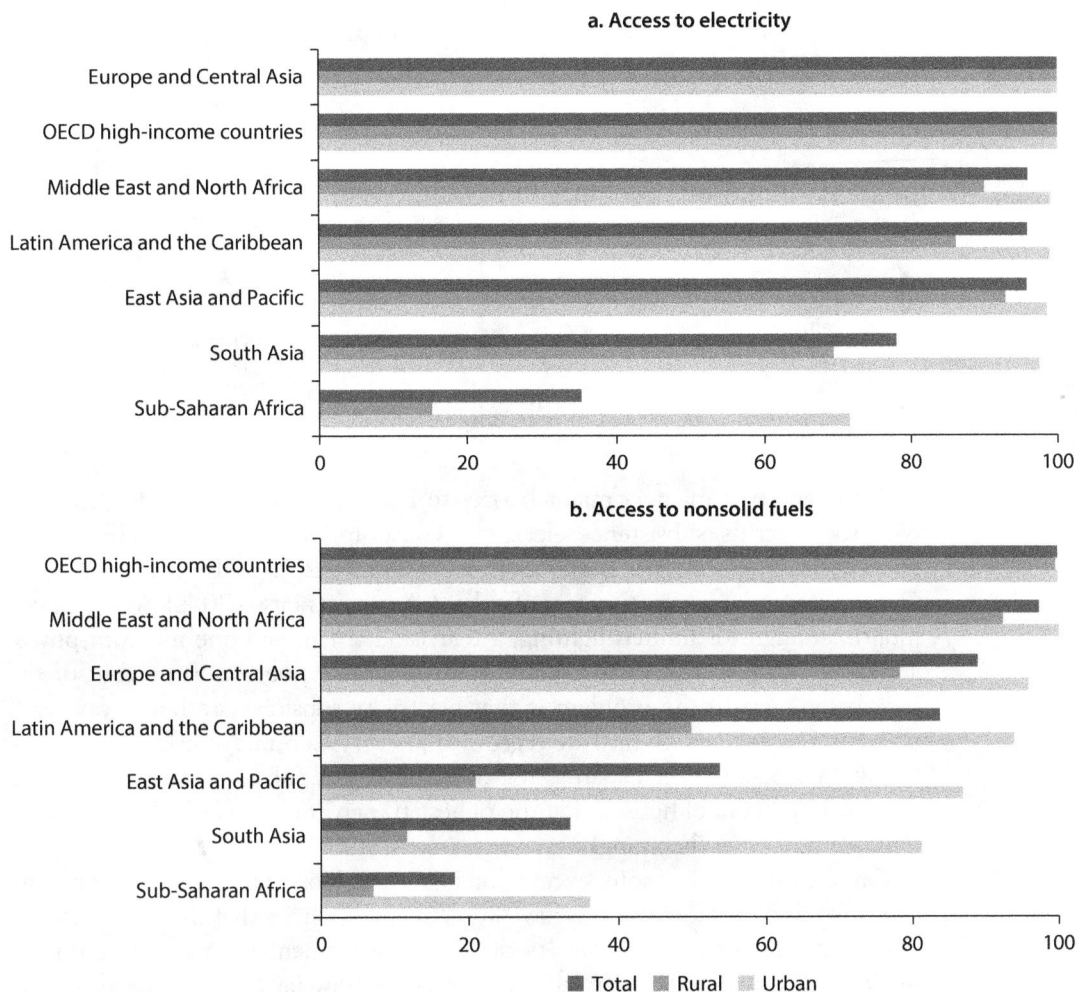

a. Access to electricity

b. Access to nonsolid fuels

Source: World Development Indicators.
Note: OECD = Organisation for Economic Co-operation and Development.

electricity supplies. Low quality of life, severe health problems, poor education and medical care, and limited opportunities for raising incomes and living standards are associated with a lack of electricity and nonsolid fuels.

The need for cleaner, more efficient cooking has not received enough policy and financial support in the region. More than half of the population in Guatemala, Honduras, and Nicaragua use solid fuel for cooking. Even in relatively wealthy Mexico, this share is 14 percent. These levels are worrisome given the association between indoor air pollution and acute lower respiratory infection and chronic obstructive pulmonary disease, 2 of the top 10 causes of death in Latin America (IHME and World Bank 2013).

Figure 1.22 Access Deficits Are Concentrated in a Few Countries, 2012
Percentage of regional total

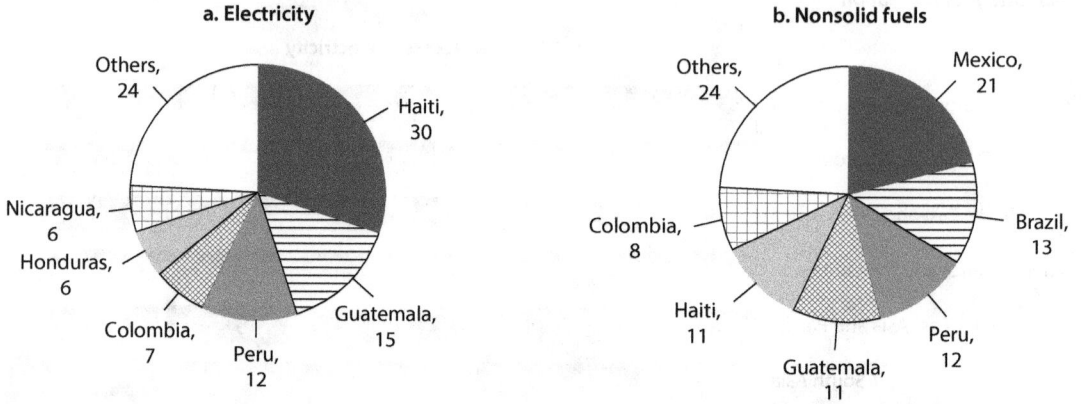

a. Electricity

Others, 24
Haiti, 30
Nicaragua, 6
Honduras, 6
Colombia, 7
Peru, 12
Guatemala, 15

b. Nonsolid fuels

Others, 24
Mexico, 21
Colombia, 8
Brazil, 13
Haiti, 11
Peru, 12
Guatemala, 11

Source: World Development Indicators.

Affordability remains a major barrier to increased access to electricity. Even with social tariffs, subsistence electricity consumption is not affordable to the poor in many Latin American countries (figure 1.23). In Bolivia, Colombia, Guatemala, and Mexico, the cost of subsistence electricity—30 kilowatt-hours a month, enough for limited lighting, a television, a fan, and one medium-power appliance—imposes an unacceptable burden for the poorest 40 percent of the population. Part of the problem is that electricity subsidies are not always well targeted. Electricity subsidies are regressive in every Central American country—to give an example, in Panama, for every US$1 of subsidies received by the poorest 10 percent of households, the richest 10 percent gets US$4.4 (Hernandez Ore and others, forthcoming).

On a more positive note, except for Haiti and Honduras, countries with the lowest levels of electricity access have implemented policies that should increase it. The energy access pillar of the Readiness for Investment in Sustainable Energy (RISE) index, which includes indicators to assess how far countries have gone in introducing the key policies, regulations, and plans needed to increase energy access and attract private participation (based on current good practice), shows most Latin American countries to be doing well. But Haiti, with energy access levels similar to those in Afghanistan and Somalia, is still lacking the core elements of an energy access program (an officially approved electrification plan, a framework for grid electrification, or even a framework for off-grid electrification based on stand-alone systems). Honduras has also progressed slowly on all these fronts, with policy and planning instruments that consider some good practice elements but not all.

A Gap Remains between the World's Best Performers and Latin America's Major Utilities

Latin America pioneered electricity market reforms and what became known as the orthodoxy of the 1990s (unbundle, privatize, regulate). As a result, several

Figure 1.23 In Many Latin American Countries, the Poorest Cannot Afford Electricity
Affordability, percentage of bottom 40 percent household income

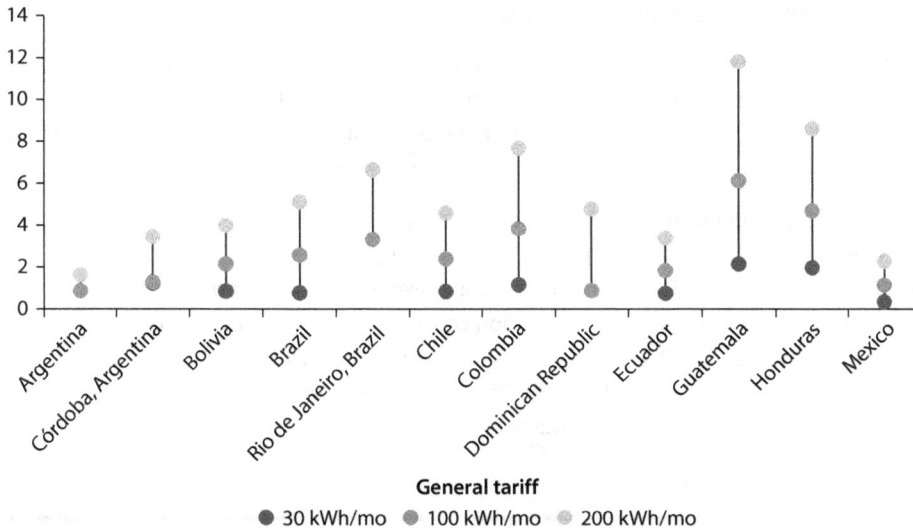

General tariff
● 30 kWh/mo ● 100 kWh/mo ● 200 kWh/mo

Source: World Bank, forthcoming a, based on SEDLAC (Socio-Economic Database for Latin America and the Caribbean) household surveys, data for 2015.
Note: Affordability is measured in the annual cost of subsistence consumption as a percentage of bottom 40 percent household income. The analysis is based on national social tariffs (and not on special programs applying to subnational levels). Electricity is generally considered affordable if annual expenditure on a volume of subsistence consumption is less than or equal to 5 percent of income. Preliminary work from World Bank Energy Global Practice. kWh = kilowatt hours.

countries in the region have highly sophisticated electricity markets, with good governance and regulatory certainty. More generally, most countries in the region have functional electricity markets, and the region has built a wealth of experience with the design and operation of electricity markets (box 1.5).

The reforms strengthened the performance of many utilities, some of which have grown to become multinational companies or at least companies able to sell shares through stock markets to finance their investment plans (such as ISA, the state-controlled electricity grid operator of Colombia, Empresas Públicas de Medellín). But a few still struggle with service quality and financial sustainability. That may be due to the reversal of reforms in some countries or to the lack of managerial expertise in some utilities. And overall, there is still a gap between most Latin American utilities and global best performers (figure 1.24).

Electricity Is Clean but Vulnerable to Climate Shocks and Still Has Lots to Gain from "Negawatts"

With 56 percent of installed electricity generating capacity in renewable sources, Latin America has the world's cleanest electricity sector. But much of this depends on hydroelectricity, which has suffered from droughts brought on by climate change and poor water resource management. As a result, the share of electricity produced from renewable sources has been falling in recent years, reaching 53 percent in 2013 (figure 1.25). In January 2015, São Paolo's

Box 1.5 Latin America Has Pioneered Innovations to Make Markets More Economically and Technically Efficient

Successful electricity reforms in Latin America are a testament to the sophistication of the region's professionals and institutions and their willingness and ability to embrace change. Examples of adjustments and innovations that moved markets to increased competition and efficiency include:

- Colombia pioneered the auctioning of reliability payments to ensure the availability of energy during dry periods and El Niño events through regulatory adjustments.
- Argentina, Brazil, and Peru introduced competitive tenders or auctions for concessions to ensure the timely addition of transmission capacity, and successfully separated ownership from operations, whereby transmission belongs to multiple owners.
- Peru and Brazil from 2009 (followed by Chile in 2015 and Mexico in 2016) launched auctions to scale up nonconventional renewable energy.

Source: World Bank, forthcoming a.

Figure 1.24 A Few Latin American Utilities Are among the Best, but Most Are Less Reliable than the Global Median Performer, 2015

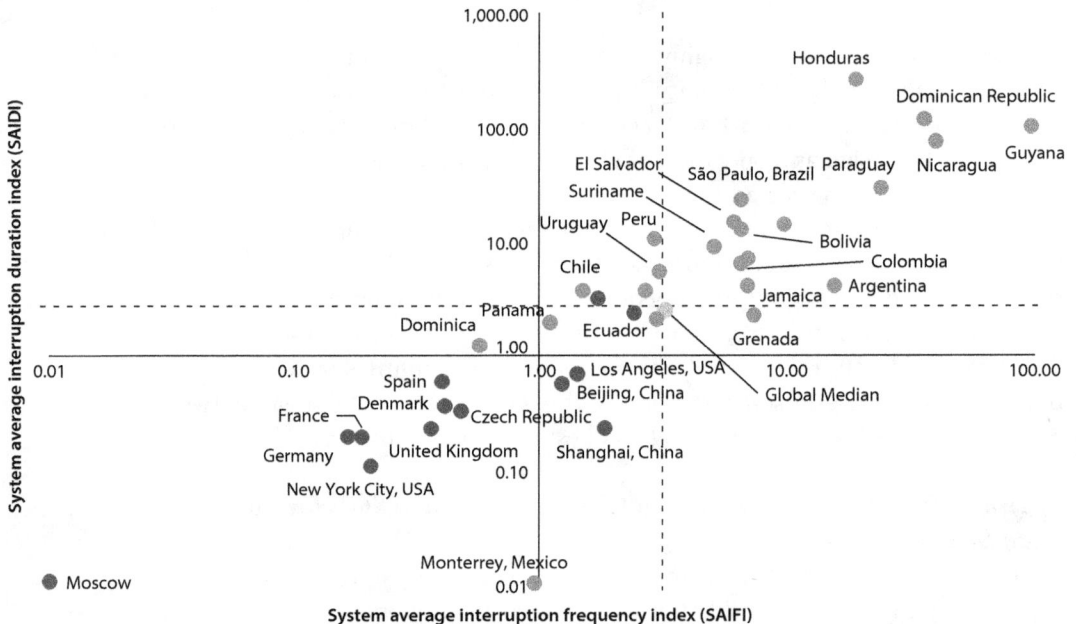

Source: World Bank 2017.
Note: Axes are in log scale. SAIDI is the average outage duration for each customer served on a yearly basis, measured in minutes. SAIFI is commonly used as a reliability indicator by power utilities and is the average number of interruptions that a customer experiences in a given year. This dataset measures SAIDI and SAIFI scores for the largest utility from the largest business city, unless otherwise noted. Orange dots are for Latin American utilities, while blue ones are for the country noted.

Figure 1.25 Among Regions, Latin America Has the Largest Share of Electricity Produced from Renewables, but This Share Has Been Declining because of Droughts, 2001–13
Percentage of electricity produced by renewable sources

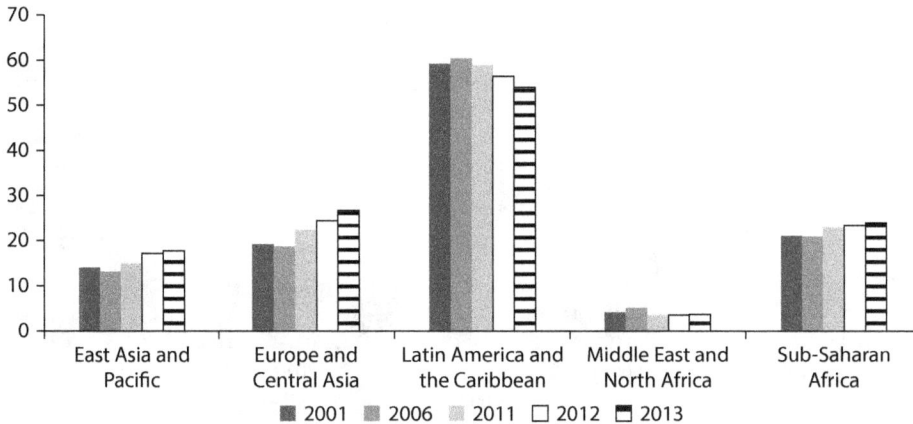

■ 2001 ■ 2006 ▨ 2011 □ 2012 ▤ 2013

Source: http://data.worldbank.org/products/wdi.

six-reservoir hydroelectric system fell below 3 percent of its 264 billion gallon capacity, forcing blackouts throughout the region (Poindexter 2015). Reservoir expansion in the region may be difficult given the mounting opposition to large hydroelectric projects, including the 11.2 gigawatt Belo Monte project in Brazil's Amazon as well as Chile's five-dam HidroAysen project (Tissot 2012). Other forms of renewable energy—geothermal, solar, tidal, wind, biomass, and biofuels— contribute only a sliver of electricity production in the region (10 percent in 2013) and have ramped up too slowly to offset the decline of hydroelectricity.

While nonhydro renewables are a rather new phenomenon in Latin America, such investments are rising. The region has seen rapid growth in solar photovoltaic (PV) plants, with a doubling of regional capacity in 2015—though from a low baseline. Similarly, onshore wind investments have been growing since 2008 (figure 1.26). Significant small hydropower and bioenergy investments are made every year, while geothermal investment appears irregularly, with a limited number of projects under development in the region. Private investment in renewables has also gradually increased in the region, mostly to support wind-based generation and mainly concentrated in Brazil, Chile, Mexico, and Peru. (Colombia, Ecuador, Uruguay, and Central American countries also attracted modest private sector investment in renewable energy in 2008–14.)

With its reliance on renewables and vulnerability to climate shocks, Latin America would benefit enormously from good regional interconnections. But many existing interconnections are not used because of technical, regulatory, and market barriers.[8] For example, regional power trade in Central America, including interconnection with Mexico, was just 2–4 percent of potential trading capacity in 2012 and 2013. Power exchanges between Argentina, Brazil, and Uruguay have also been consistently low. Electrons are not flowing across borders—or at least, many fewer than there could be.

Figure 1.26 Investments in Renewables Are Rising Rapidly in Latin America, Driven by Onshore Wind
US$ billions

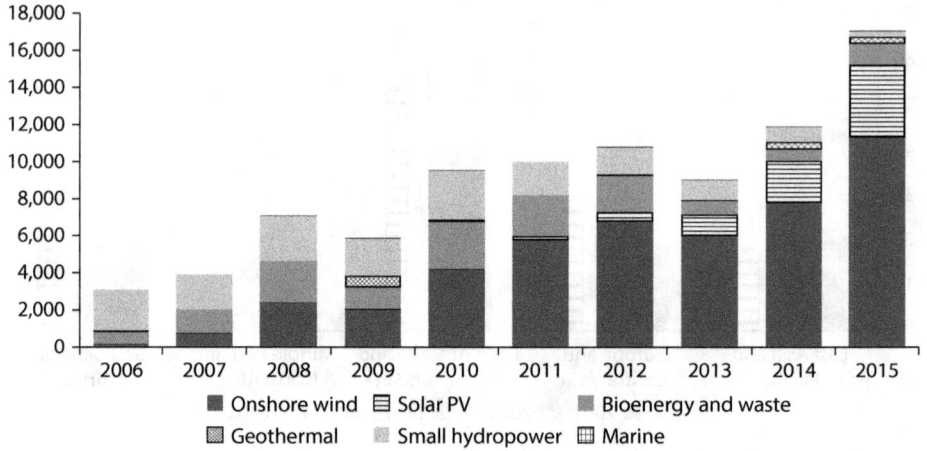

Source: World Bank, forthcoming a.
Note: Includes both public and private investment. Hydropower larger than 50 megawatts is not covered by the analysis but is expected to remain the dominant technology for further renewable energy deployment in the region in the long term. PV = photovoltaic.

Figure 1.27 The Region's Transmission and Distribution Losses Are Some of the Highest in the World, 2001–13
Percentage

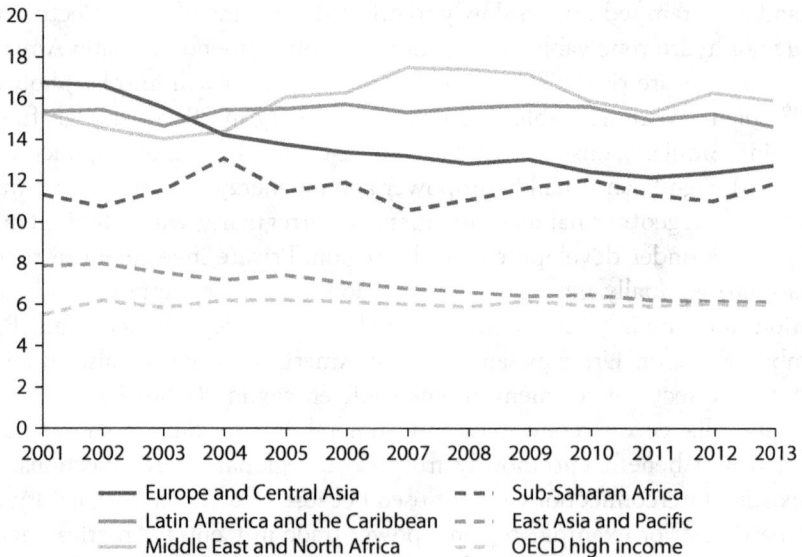

Source: World Bank, forthcoming a.
Note: OECD = Organisation for Economic Co-operation and Development.

Another factor that could help the region keep its low energy emission footprint, as well as reduce vulnerability, would be increased energy efficiency. Latin America's energy intensity is the lowest of any region, largely because of the nature of its economic activities. But energy efficiency, particularly in the use of fossil fuels, remains poor. And the region could reduce transmission and distribution losses, which are the highest of any region except the Middle East and North Africa (and three times those of East Asia; figure 1.27).

Conclusions

One way to interpret the diagnostic laid out above is to argue that Latin America's infrastructure performance is rather mediocre for an upper-middle-income region with significant growth aspirations. Another is to highlight the many examples of the region's capacity for innovative solutions, its expertise with sophisticated regulations, and its experience with PPPs. In sum, Latin America has the means and potential to do better. And it can do so by spending more efficiently on the right things.

So, where to go with this diagnostic? The next section turns to the challenges and opportunities that will shape how Latin America can or should tackle its infrastructure agenda.

Notes

1. Henceforth we use Latin America as shorthand for Latin America and the Caribbean.

2. Brazil represents about 44 percent of the region's GDP, Mexico about 25 percent, and Argentina 10 percent.

3. Based on data from Ruiz-Nuñez (2016).

4. Governments can offer indirect support through guarantees to reduce specific project risks—for example, payment, revenue, and exchange rate guarantees. They can also provide direct support to deals from their budgets in case user fees or power or water purchase agreements with private entities or wholesale markets are not possible or sufficient (in some cases, government may collect user fees but provide availability payments to the private entities bearing the demand risk).

5. See, for example, research cited in Ali and others (2015) that used high-resolution imagery to analyze the impact of new road construction on deforestation in Brazil (Laurance, Goosem, and Laurance 2009) and Bolivia, Panama, Paraguay, and Peru (Reymondin and others 2013).

6. Based on BRTdata.org, urbanrail.net, metrobits.org, and UNDESA (2014).

7. This share is inferred by looking at the share of the urban population that lives in slums and other informal settlements that utilities may not be allowed to serve.

8. The region has four clusters of interconnection: Mexico-United States, Central America, Andean Community (Colombia, Ecuador, Peru, República Bolivariana de Venezuela), and Southern Cone (Argentina, Brazil, Paraguay, and Uruguay).

References

Ali, Rubaba, A. Federico Barra, Claudia Berg, Richard Damania, John Nash, and Jason Russ. 2015. *Highways to Success or Byways to Waste: Estimating the Economic Benefits of Roads in Africa*. Washington, DC: World Bank. https://openknowledge.worldbank .org/handle/10986/22551.

Balbotín, Patricio Rozas, and Liliana Salazar Arredondo. 2015. "Violencia de género en el transporte público: Una regulación pendiente." Recursos Naturales e Infraestructura 172, Comisión Económica para América Latina y el Caribe, United Nations, Santiago. http://www.cepal.org/es/publicaciones/38862-violencia-genero-transporte -publico-regulacion-pendiente.

Bhattacharya, Amar, Mattia Romani, and Nicholas Stern. 2012. "Infrastructure for Development: Meeting the Challenge." Policy paper, Centre for Climate Change Economics and Policy and Grantham Research Institute on Climate Change and the Environment, London, June. http://www.lse.ac.uk/GranthamInstitute/wp-content /uploads/2014/03/PP-infrastructure-for-development-meeting-the-challenge.pdf.

Borja-Vega, Christian, Gustavo Perochena, and Virginia Zuilu. 2015. "Infrastructure for Sharing Prosperity in Latin American and the Caribbean Region (LAC) Water and Sanitation." World Bank, Washington, DC.

CAF (Banco de Desarollo de América Latina). 2011. *IDeAL 2011. La infraestructura en el desarrollo integral de América Latina. Diagnóstico estratégico y propuestas para una agenda prioritaria. Agua potable y saneamiento*. IDeAL, Caracas: CAF. http://scioteca .caf.com/handle/123456789/347.

———. 2013. *IDeAL 2013. La infraestructura en el desarrollo integral de América Latina. Fortalecer las capacidades logísticas y competir exitosamente en los mercados mundiales de servicios logísticos: imperativos y oportunidades para América Latina*. IDeAL, Caracas: CAF. http://scioteca.caf.com/handle/123456789/354. de Fomento. https://www.caf .com/_custom/static/ideal_2013/assets/book_1.pdf.

CAF (Corporación Andina de Fomento). 2014. *Encuesta de hogares 2013: Principales resultados*. Bogotá: CAF. http://scioteca.caf.com/handle/123456789/409.

Crabtree, Tom, Tom Hoang, Jim Edgar, and Russell Tom. 2015. "World Air Cargo Forecast, 2014–2015." Boeing, Seattle.

Cubas, Diana, Maria Claudia Pachón, Tatiana Peralta, Xijie Lu, and Steven Farji. 2015. "Access to Transport Infrastructure and Services." Background paper commissioned for this report, World Bank, Washington, DC.

Dulac, John. 2013. "Infrastructure Requirements: Estimating Road and Railway Infrastructure Capacity and Costs to 2050." Information paper, International Energy Agency, Paris. https://www.iea.org/publications/freepublications/publication/Transpo rtInfrastructureInsights_FINAL_WEB.pdf.

Fay, Marianne. 2001. "Financing the Future: Infrastructure Needs in Latin America, 2000–05." Policy Research Working Paper 2545, World Bank, Washington, DC. https://openknowledge.worldbank.org/handle/10986/19965.

Fay, Marianne, and Mary Morrison. 2007. *Infrastructure in Latin America and the Caribbean: Recent Developments and Key Challenges*. Washington, DC: World Bank.

Fay, Marianne, and Tito Yepes. 2003. "Investing in Infrastructure: What Is Needed from 2000 to 2010?" Policy Research Working Paper 3102, World Bank, Washington, DC. https://openknowledge.worldbank.org/handle/10986/18147.

Gwilliams, Kenneth. 2012. "Practical Indicators for Comparing and Evaluating Subsidy Instruments." World Bank, Washington, DC.

Hernandez Ore, Marco Antonio, Luis Alvaro Sanchez, Liliana D. Sousa, and Leopoldo Tornarolli. Forthcoming. *Fiscal and Welfare Impacts of Electricity Subsidies in Central America*. Washington, DC: World Bank.

Hidalgo, Darío. 2011. "Transporte sostenible para América Latina: Situación actual y perspectivas." Prepared for the Sustainable Transport Forum of Latin America, Bogotá, June 22–24.

IDB (Inter-American Development Bank). 2015. *Freight Transport and Logistics Yearbook, 2014*. Washington, DC: IDB. https://publications.iadb.org/handle/11319/6885.

IHME (Institute for Health Metrics and Evaluation) and World Bank. 2013. *The Global Burden of Disease: Generating Evidence, Guiding Policy—Latin America and Caribbean Regional Edition*. Seattle: IHME. http://www.healthdata.org/sites/default/files/files /policy_report/2013/WB_LatinAmericaCaribbean/IHME_GBD_WorldBank _LatinAmericaCaribbean_FullReport.pdf.

ITF (International Transport Federation). 2015. "Urban Passenger Transport Scenarios for Latin America, China, and India." In *Transport Outlook 2015*, 91–138. Organisation for Economic Co-operation and Development, Paris. http://www.oecd-ilibrary.org /content/book/9789282107782-en.

———. 2016. "Capacity to Grow: Transport Infrastructure Needs for Future Trade Growth." Organisation for Economic Co-operation and Development, Paris. http:// www.itf-oecd.org/sites/default/files/docs/future-growth-transport-infrastructure .pdf.

Jaimurzina, Azhar, Gabriel Pérez Salas, and Ricardo J. Sánchez. 2015. "Políticas de logística y movilidad para el desarrollo sostenible y la integración regional." Recursos Naturales e Infraestructura 174, Comisión Económica para América Latina y el Caribe, United Nations, Santiago.

Jirón, Paola. 2013. "Sustainable Urban Mobility in Latin America and the Caribbean." Thematic study prepared for *Planning and Design for Sustainable Urban Mobility: Global Report on Human Settlements 2013*. United Nations Human Settlements Programme, Nairobi. http://unhabitat.org/wp-content/uploads/2013/06/GRHS.2013 .Regional.Latin_.America.and_.Caribbean.pdf.

Kohli, Harpaul Alberto, and Phillip Basil. 2011. "Requirements for Infrastructure Investment in Latin America under Alternate Growth Scenarios, 2011–2040." *Global Journal of Emerging Market Economies* 3 (1): 59–110.

Laurance, William F., Miriam Goosem, and Susan G. W. Laurance. 2009. "Impacts of Roads and Linear Clearings on Tropical Forests." *Trends in Ecology and Evolution* 24 (12): 659–69.

Mehndiratta, Shomik, Camila Rodriguez, and Catalina Ochoa. 2014. "Targeted Subsidies in Public Transport: Combining Affordability with Financial Sustainability." World Bank, Washington, DC.

Nolasco, Daniel. 2016. *Report on Current Wastewater Treatment Trends in LAC*. Oshawa, ON: Nolasco & Associates.

OECD (Organisation for Economic Co-operation and Development) and ECLAC (Economic Commission for Latin America and the Caribbean). 2012. *Latin American Economic Outlook 2012: Transforming the State for Development*. Paris: OECD.

Osborne, Theresa, Maria Claudia Pachón, and Gonzalo Enrique Araya. 2014. "What Drives the High Price of Road Freight Transport in Central America?" Policy Research Working Paper 6844, World Bank, Washington, DC. http://documents.worldbank.org /curated/en/364161468212970549/pdf/WPS6844.pdf.

Perrotti, Daniel E., and Ricardo J. Sánchez. 2011. "La brecha de infraestructura en América Latina y el Caribe." Recursos Naturales e Infraestructura 153, Comisión Económica para América Latina y el Caribe, United Nations, Santiago.

Poindexter, Gregory B. 2015. "Brazil's Drought Brings Water Supply to Near Zero Capacity at Hydroelectric Facilities." Renewable Energy World, January 29.

Poveda, Stalin. 2014. "Investigación y diagnostico social para la universalización de las conexiones intradomiciliarias de alcantarillado sanitario del subsistema sur de Guayaquil." World Bank, Washington, DC.

Powell, Andrew, ed. 2013. Rethinking Reforms: How Latin America and the Caribbean Can Escape Suppressed World Growth. Washington, DC: Inter-American Development Bank. http://www19.iadb.org/intal/intalcdi/PE/2013/11625en.pdf.

Reymondin, Louis, Karolina Argote, Andy Jarvis, Carolina Navarrete, Alejandro Coca, Denny Grossman, Alberto Villalba, and Paul Suding. 2013. "Road Impact Assessment Using Remote Sensing Methodology for Monitoring Land-Use Change in Latin America: Results of Five Case Studies." Technical Note IDB-TN-561, Inter-American Development Bank, Washington, DC.

Rodriguez, Camila, Juan Miguel Gallego, Daniel Martínez, Sergio Montoya, and Tatiana Peralta-Quiros. 2016. "Examining the Implementation and Labor Outcomes of Targeted Transit Subsidies: SISBEN Subsidy for Bogotá's Urban Poor." World Bank, Washington, DC.

Ruiz-Nuñez, Fernanda. 2016. "Overview of Infrastructure Finance in LAC (Selected Graphs)." World Bank, Washington, DC.

Ruiz-Nuñez, Fernanda, and Zichao Wei. 2015. "Infrastructure Investment Demands in Emerging Markets and Developing Economies." Policy Research Working Paper 7414, World Bank, Washington, DC.

Serebrisky, Tomás. 2011. Airport Economics in Latin America and the Caribbean: Benchmarking, Regulation, and Pricing. Washington, DC: World Bank.

Serebrisky, Tomás, Andrés Gómez-Lobo, Nicolás Estupiñán, and Ramón Muñoz-Raskin. 2009. "Affordability and Subsidies in Public Urban Transport: What Do We Mean, What Can Be Done?" Transport Reviews 29 (6): 715–39.

Serebrisky, Tomás, Ancor Suárez-Alemán, Diego Margot, and Maria Cecilia Ramirez. 2015. "Financing Infrastructure in Latin America and the Caribbean: How, How Much, and by Whom?" Inter-American Development Bank, Washington, DC. https:// publications.iadb.org/bitstream/handle/11319/7315/Infrastructure%20 Financing.%20Definitivo.pdf?sequence=1.

Shankland, Alex, Ken Caplan, Ivan Paiva, Klaus Neder, Hernán Gómez Bruera, and Luciana Lupo. 2010. Global Economic and Sector Work (ESW) on the Political Economy of Sanitation in Four Countries. Washington, DC: World Bank.

Tissot, Roger. 2012. "Latin America's Energy Future." Discussion Paper 252, Inter-American Development Bank, Washington, DC.

TomTom International. 2015. "TomTom Traffic Index: Measuring Congestion Worldwide." https://www.tomtom.com/en_gb/trafficindex/list.

TransMilenio. 2015. "Beneficios de transporte para personas sisbenizadas." http://www
.sitp.gov.co/publicaciones/beneficios_de_transporte_para_personas_sisbenizadas.

UNDESA (United Nations Department of Economic and Social Affairs). 2014. "World
Urbanization Prospects: The 2014 Revision." United Nations, New York. https://esa
.un.org/unpd/wpp/.

UN-Habitat (United Nations Human Settlements Programme). 2013. *Planning and Design
for Sustainable Urban Mobility: Global Report on Human Settlements 2013*. New York:
Routledge. http://unhabitat.org/?mbt_book=planning-and-design-for-sustainable
-urban-mobility-global-report-on-human-settlements-2013.

WEF (World Economic Forum). 2015. *The Global Competitiveness Report* 2015–2016.
Geneva: WEF. http://reports.weforum.org/global-competitiveness-report-2015-2016/.

WHO (World Health Organization) and UNICEF (United Nations Children's Fund).
2016. *Twenty-Five Years: Progress on Sanitation and Drinking Water—2015 Update and
MDG Assessment*. Geneva: WHO and UNICEF. http://www.who.int/water
_sanitation_health/publications/jmp-2015-update/en/.

World Bank. 2015. "Peru: Support to the Subnational Transport Program Project."
World Bank, Washington, DC. http://documents.worldbank.org/curated/en
/117951494238205262/Peru-LATIN-AMERICA-AND-CARIBBEAN-P132515
-Support-to-the-Subnational-Transport-Program-Project-Procurement-Plan.

———. 2016. *Doing Business 2016: Measuring Regulatory Quality and Efficiency*.
Washington, DC: World Bank.

———. 2017. *Doing Business 2017: Equal Opportunity for All*. Washington, DC:
World Bank.

———. Forthcoming a. *Energy Markets in LAC: Emerging Disruptions and the Next
Frontier*. Washington, DC: World Bank.

———. Forthcoming b. *Strengthening Governance in Infrastructure in Brazil*. Washington,
DC: World Bank.

CHAPTER 2

What Lies Ahead for the Region's Infrastructure?

Latin America faces many challenges and opportunities as it contemplates where and how to improve its infrastructure. Some of these are new, such as climate change and the policy and technology shifts associated with it. Others, such as urbanization and a growing middle class, have been long in the making but have reached a scale that puts the region in a different realm of demand and delivery options. And others are familiar, such as the fiscal space challenge and generally poor spending efficiency that have long plagued Latin America.

Inefficient Public Spending May Limit How Much More *Should* Go to Infrastructure

A recent analysis of infrastructure governance in Brazil concluded that "creating additional space for investment may not lead to economic growth or better infrastructure services, unless the management of capital projects is considerably improved" (World Bank, forthcoming b, 3). And while in-depth analysis of infrastructure planning and investment frameworks is rare—in Latin America and elsewhere—it is possible to glean insights from both public expenditure and investment management analysis and the 20 or so reasonably recent World Bank public expenditures reviews that have addressed at least one infrastructure sector. (See appendix A for a list.)

A review of these works shows that inefficient public spending on infrastructure in Latin America has myriad causes. Many of the causes lie outside infrastructure sectors or are systemic across government agencies—but all converge around a lack of institutional capacity for planning, capital budgeting, and implementation. Issues include weak appraisal and preparation capacity, overly rigid budgeting rules designed to control cash expenditures rather than improve spending efficiency, difficulties with budget execution, inefficient procurement procedures, and a systemic bias against capital spending. Many of these causes are compounded by limited coordination between sector agencies and central and subnational governments. These points, developed below, suggest substantial potential for efficiency gains.

Weak Planning, Project Appraisal, and Preparation Capacity

Public investment management systems are inefficient across the region, though some countries are better than others. Most countries have public investment management systems whose original goal was to standardize capital budget preparation by setting legal procedures for project identification and budgeting. A World Bank/IMF Public Investment Management index (PIMI) (Dabla-Norris and others 2012) found that Latin America has low investment efficiency, with significant variations across countries, mainly determined by how old systems are. The study analyzed four stages of infrastructure management—appraisal (including planning), selection, implementation, and evaluation—and found appraisal and evaluation to be the weakest stages. A 2016 study reached similar conclusions (Armendáriz and Contreras 2016).

Longer-term infrastructure planning is undermined by short-term pressures. The region's public investment management systems were built with a strong focus on managing fiscal deficits and, therefore, maintaining strong controls on actual cash expenditure. There is a disconnect between decentralized project planning responsibilities in sector agencies and overall fiscal targets and plans. This disconnect emerges because agencies develop plans separately from budget discussions. For example, a 2015 World Bank perception survey of project managers in Jamaica concluded that only 13 percent of government projects were aligned with a high-level strategic goal.[1] In Haiti, a lack of coordination among key agencies and the absence of an integrated budget are major challenges. Whereas the country has a detailed, comprehensive budget cycle for investments, the budget still fails to incorporate long-term decision making in several ways.

Another issue is the complex interplay between politics and planning. Spending efficiently requires a sober assessment of any project's net benefits to society. Projects should be prioritized against each other, across sectors, and over time—thereby turning wish lists into strategies. That approach requires a political mandate, a process for generating such a mandate, and institutional capacity to manage such a process (in an infrastructure unit, the ministry of finance or planning, or the president's office). Key, however, is a robust public investment management process that ensures quality.

However, a lack of public investment management-based quality control leads to projects being funded that are not sufficiently prepared. A 2014 United Nations–Economic Commission for Latin America and the Caribbean survey of 15 Latin American economies found that in 5 countries, public-private partnership (PPP) projects can bypass public investment management system controls, while in 4 more, significant exceptions can be obtained (Perrotti and Rueda 2015). Brazil has a multiyear planning process, but it is seen more as a bureaucratic burden than as an instrument for medium-term planning (World Bank, forthcoming b). In addition, parliamentary amendments to annual budget laws can add substantially to planned investments (some 33 percent in 2015). A recent study consequently concludes that "the combination of weak capacity, lax enforcement, and pork-barrel politics means that investment projects can be included in ministerial budgets without having been subject to formal appraisal" (World Bank, forthcoming b).

In terms of quality control, the situation is often worse at the subnational level. States and municipalities frequently face a lack of human and technical capacity to manage large-scale investments. The state of Rio de Janeiro has a multiannual plan to guide its investment decisions, but day-to-day decisions are at the mercy of political and sectoral considerations that lead to ad hoc budget allocations (World Bank 2012a). Subnational levels sometimes follow national level guidelines and manuals for project appraisal without properly understanding them. In addition, subnational levels often see the use of national guidelines and manuals as a purely formal prerequisite for applying for national funding rather than as a way to strengthen their own decision-making process.[2]

Overly Rigid or Myopic Budgeting

In the region, annual budget rules limit the inclusion of large and long-term projects. Most public investment projects are funded on an annual basis, meaning these projects need to be executed in less than a year according to tight fiscal calendars. Of over 23 Latin American countries that had Public Expenditure and Financial Accountability (PEFA) analysis done since 2006, only one got an A rating (Colombia) on the PEFA indicator that captures the existence of sector strategies with multiyear costing of recurrent and investment expenditure (table 2.1). Out of a portfolio of 42,810 projects registered in Bolivia's project data bank (SISIN) until 2013, nearly 70 percent were for two years or less. Less than 1 percent of Peru's nearly 220,000 public projects registered between 2000 and 2015 at national and subnational levels had a duration of three or more years.

There is growing realization that this is an issue, and some countries are working on reforms. Colombia, for example, has a strong planning system and has introduced medium-term expenditures frameworks. However, it still has a complex process for multiannual budget allocations for projects that requires approval by a specialized committee and dedicated cabinet approval.

Further, the effectiveness of budget allocations is limited by a lack of information about and timeliness of financial flows to projects. This hampers project managers' capacity to do financial planning during project implementation stages. In Jamaica, the same survey of project managers found that over 70 percent of projects received information about financial flows three months or less before scheduled project start. In Mexico's water sector, unwieldy budgetary rules squeeze the budget cycle in a way that makes it difficult to engage in multiyear budgeting and properly execute capital budgets. This is because resources are not released until a technical agreement is signed between the federal water agency and participating states—expected by March 31 but

Table 2.1 Only One Latin American Country Fares Well with Respect to the Multiyear Budgeting of Projects

Latest available year, 2007–13

Bolivia	D
Brazil	C
Colombia	A
Costa Rica	D
Dominican Republic	C
El Salvador	D
Grenada	D
Guatemala	C
Haiti	D
Honduras	D
Jamaica	C
Paraguay	D
Peru	C
Trinidad and Tobago	D

Source: PEFA Secretariat.

Note: Table shows scores for ID-12 indicator (iii): Existence of sector strategies with multiyear costing of recurrent expenditure and investment. Scores are from A (best) to D (worst).

sometimes delayed—and any resources unspent by December 31 must be returned. This tight schedule results in less competitive procurement procedures and low budget execution (World Bank 2014b).

Finally, the fiscal calendar is often misaligned with the project implementation calendar. The Latin American fiscal year is the calendar year, which results in fiscal authorities requesting deliverables and payments before the end of the year. However, for most infrastructure projects, the right time to do investment is during the dry or summer season that happens between November and March. In response, some countries have created fiduciary funds to avoid this budget rigidity, while others chose PPPs or struggled with multiannual allocations.

Difficulties with Budget Execution

Many countries struggle with the execution of capital budgets (figure 2.1). This is a particular issue in Brazil where disbursement data show a chronic gap between committed and executed funds. This problem was exacerbated by the transformation of the Pilot Program of Investments into the much more ambitious Program of Growth Acceleration, which increased public investments from 0.7 of gross domestic product (GDP) in 2007 to 1.3 percent in 2012. In 2013, the Federal Audit Court found that a third of road construction and management projects were paralyzed for a variety of reasons, and three-quarters of projects with fully committed funds had an execution rate of less than 25 percent. The court also found serious irregularities in 58 of the 102 large infrastructure projects it audited (World Bank, forthcoming b).

Figure 2.1 Many Latin American Countries Chronically Underexecute Their Capital Investment Budget

Disbursement as percentage of commitment

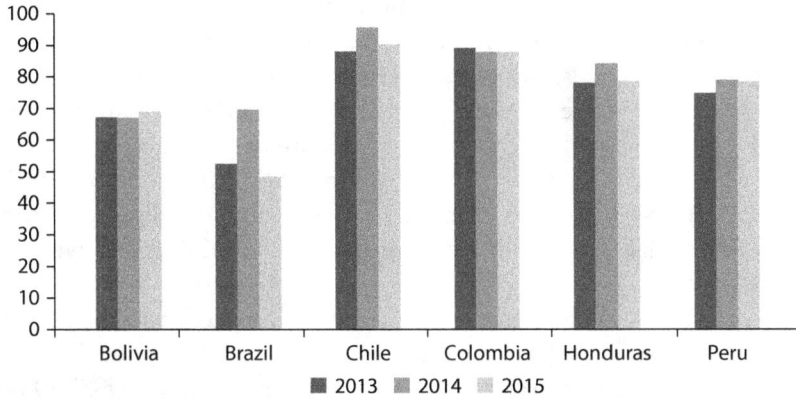

Source: Courtesy of Diego Dorado, based on data from government budgetary reporting systems (Bolivia: VIPFE; Brazil: SIOP; Chile DIPRES; Colombia: Portal de Transparencia; Honduras: SIAFI; Peru: http://www.mef.go.pe/estadisticas).

Low- or medium-level budget execution has many causes. For example, in Honduras, cash rationing is considered the main driver of low budget execution in infrastructure investments, as money is siphoned off to protect current expenditures. Furthermore, budget execution is defined as accrued expenses rather than actual payments, resulting in perpetually overstated budget capacity (World Bank 2013a).

Chronic overexecution is also symptomatic of poor budgeting. In Guatemala, the budgetary requirements of the perpetually underfunded road ministry were estimated in 2010 to be four times its US$1 billion budget. These funding requirements include projects that are approved but not executed, as well as projects executed but where the contractor has not yet been paid for its work. To compensate for the lack of funds, the ministry often receives transfers from ministries that have more funds than they can fully execute. That, combined with frequent cost overruns in road projects, led the road ministry to execute 120–200 percent of its budget between 2006 and 2008 (World Bank 2013d). This effectively undermines the annual budget process' ability to guide fiscal policy.

Procurement That Could Be Improved

Inefficient procurement processes contribute to limited budget execution. Capital expenditures depend on procurement policies for the timely provision of goods and services. Some procurement or budget laws do not allow agencies to start the procurement process before a budget appropriation has been given. This causes unnecessary delays. In Jamaica, the project manager survey revealed that 76 percent of the projects faced delays on the implementation of their procurement plans.

In addition, better procurement could save significant resources in many Latin American countries. For example, it is estimated that Costa Rica could have saved 13–18 percent of its 2008 budget by taking advantage of procurement practices such as reverse auctions, consolidated purchases, and clearer standards (World Bank 2008). In Haiti, excessively high thresholds for public tendering of works, goods, and services result in overreliance on direct procurement or noncompetitive invoicing (World Bank 2016). Guatemala has no systematic procurement reviews for the procurement of goods and services, many of which occur in infrastructure sectors (World Bank 2013d). In Brazil, adjustments of 25–50 percent of initial cost estimates are allowed to preserve "economic-financial equilibrium," encouraging underbidding and overcharging (World Bank 2014a).

Some economies in the region such as Chile, Mexico, and Brazil have seen remarkable success in driving procurement reforms. In Chile for example, the ChileCompra electronic portal is estimated to have generated US$280 million in savings. Mexico's modernization of its tendering processes (which involved eliminating 586 obsolete procurement regulations and creating an online platform to boost transparency and ease of access) generated savings of more than US$1 billion within three years of its 2009 start (World Bank 2013c). In Brazil, a reform establishing an e-procurement system led to 51 percent savings in transaction costs and 25.5 percent reduction in prices between 2000 and 2006 (Hunja 2012).

But detailed analysis of procurement performance in Latin America and the Caribbean (LAC), both general and of public private partnerships, shows there is considerable room for improvement (see appendix B for a more detailed review). The region's reasonably good average performance compared to others hides wide variation both across countries and across different aspects of performance. The World Bank's *Benchmarking Public Procurement 2017* found that suppliers identify obstacles such as excessive bureaucracy and red tape in Colombia and Honduras; payment delays in Argentina, the Dominican Republic, and Jamaica; lack of transparency and opaque tendering processes in Brazil and Mexico; lack of efficiency in Barbados and Puerto Rico; the list goes on.

Insufficient Attention to Social and Environmental Risk Management

Adequate social and environmental risk management[3] helps secure popular support for a project—a "social license to operate"—which reduces business costs by reducing project delays, cost overruns, and reputational risk to investors (Stapledon 2012). Data from the Ministry of Economy and Finance of Peru showed that delays associated with land acquisition and expropriation significantly delayed projects. The ministry found that these delays caused substantial increases in project costs (table 2.2).

In Latin America, while some countries have put in place relevant policies and procedures to address sustainability in infrastructure, there is still a long road ahead. Yet when social sustainability dimensions are not clearly understood and properly analyzed, decision makers tend to ignore them until

Table 2.2 Project Delays as a Result of Land Acquisition, Expropriation, and Regulation Requirements

Project and concession	Start date	Total investment at risk (US$ millions)	Completion by 2015 in %
Jorge Chavez International Airport	2001	1,062	30.6
Red Vial No. 6. Pucusana-Cerro Azul-Ica	2005	294	36.5
Autopista del Sol-Trujillo-Sullana	2010	330	21.2
Line 2, Lima Metro	2014	5,347	4.2

Source: Ministry of Economy and Finance, Peru. Total investment refers to the initial estimated cost of the investment.

they flare up and directly threaten project implementation (Geurs, Boon, and Van Wee 2009).

Another area in which social and environmental risk management is undervalued is feasibility studies. As in other regions, feasibility studies in Latin America tend to focus on engineering as well as economic and financial analysis. They seldom make use of other tools, such as environmental and social impact assessments and stakeholder engagement, or pay due attention to Free, Prior, and Informed Consent rules.

Attention to these issues can help avoid later complications, reduce negative impacts, and compensate for any residual impacts. In the experience of the World Bank, feasibility studies sometimes fail to adequately assess project sites, unforeseen site conditions including social and economic activities, existing utilities, and, most important, contextual risk. Moreover, feasibility studies must integrate the projects' unique characteristics in order to properly analyze their potential distributional impacts on diverse social groups, both spatially and temporally. A flexible and adaptive social and environmental management system in which the level of effort to manage the risks is proportionate to the degree of the risks in the infrastructure projects improves projects' chances of success.

Unclear Project Sustainability

An imbalance between capital and current spending on infrastructure is a chronic problem around the world. It can spring from overly rigid budgets and suboptimal planning. Of the 23 Latin American countries that had PEFA analysis since 2006, only three ever got a rate of B (Guatemala, Peru, and Trinidad and Tobago) on the indicator capturing the link between investment budgets and forward expenditure estimates (table 2.3).

The imbalance is also frequently because of poor coordination between central governments that fund and often manage capital investments and local governments that may lack the financial and technical capacity to take over these investments or cover operation and maintenance costs. In Honduras, municipalities are legally mandated to invest 50–70 percent of the transfers they receive from the central government, but because transfers are unpredictable in both timing and amount, municipal leaders tend to front-load recurrent expenditures (for example, salaries and interest payments) and use whatever is

Table 2.3 Latin American Countries Score Poorly on Links between Investment Budgets and Forward Expenditure Estimates, Latest Available Years, 2007–13

Bolivia	C
Brazil	C
Colombia	C
Costa Rica	D
Dominican Republic	C
El Salvador	C
Grenada	D
Guatemala	C
Haiti	D
Honduras	C
Jamaica	C
Panama	D
Paraguay	D
Peru	B
Trinidad and Tobago	B

Source: PEFA Secretariat.
Note: Table shows scores for ID-12 indicator (iv): Links between investment budgets and forward expenditure estimates. Scores are from A (best) to D (worst).

left for investment (World Bank 2013a). Peru has the opposite problem: the fiscal responsibility law's requirement that mining revenues (canons) be dedicated to investments has led to an imbalance between capital and current expenditures in local budgets and the need for the central government to step in for critical current spending (World Bank 2012b).

A Tight Fiscal Stance Limits How Much More *Could* Be Spent on Infrastructure

Improved efficiency is not just good policy; it may well be the only option in the short to medium term to increase resources available given the region's tight fiscal position. This is not new. Fiscal constraints have long influenced both infrastructure investments and policies in the region.

Infrastructure privatization and reforms in the 1990s were largely driven by fiscal concerns. While the reforms did ease the strain on public coffers, it quickly became clear that PPPs were no substitute for public investment in infrastructure. As a result, by the early 2000s, it was clear that the region needed to invest more. But by then, Latin America was struggling with negative fiscal balances, which were raising fears of a return to hyperinflation and fiscal debacles. Pressure to limit spending combined with severe budget rigidities (typically due to a large share of the budget allocated to constitutionally mandated expenditures or to entitlements) meant that investments bore the brunt of the adjustments—even as some were arguing that infrastructure investments, being growth enhancing, should be increased. The debate raged on regarding whether fiscal space could be created at least for carefully selected growth-enhancing investments (that in turn would create more fiscal space through growth). Most countries opted not to for fear of jeopardizing credit ratings.

Indeed, evidence shows that the evolution of the public sector's budget constraint—which plays a big role in shaping fiscal space—matters for the level of infrastructure investment. Public investments in infrastructure in Latin America respond to lagged changes in public savings. However, this response is asymmetric, being stronger in good times (when lagged public savings rise) than in bad times (when lagged public savings fall) (Serebrisky and others 2015).

Many countries in Latin America are now facing persistent and often sizable fiscal deficits, which is bound to impact their ability to undertake much-needed public investments in infrastructure even with the asymmetry discussed above. The overall fiscal picture is not uniform across the region.

Public Investments in Latin America: Rising during the Boom, but Still Much Lower than in Other Regions

A narrative that has gained some traction in the region states that Latin America squandered its opportunity to invest during the boom years of 2004–08 and instead mostly expanded public consumption. That is not quite true. Total public investment (not just infrastructure related) increased by 50 percent during 2004–08, while public consumption held steady. The reverse has happened since 2009, during the crisis years, with public investment declining while consumption spending expanded (figure 2.2). However, throughout that time, public

Figure 2.2 Total Public Investments Expanded during the Boom Years while Public Consumption Remained Steady—but Public Consumption Remains Many Multiples of Public Investment

Percentage of GDP

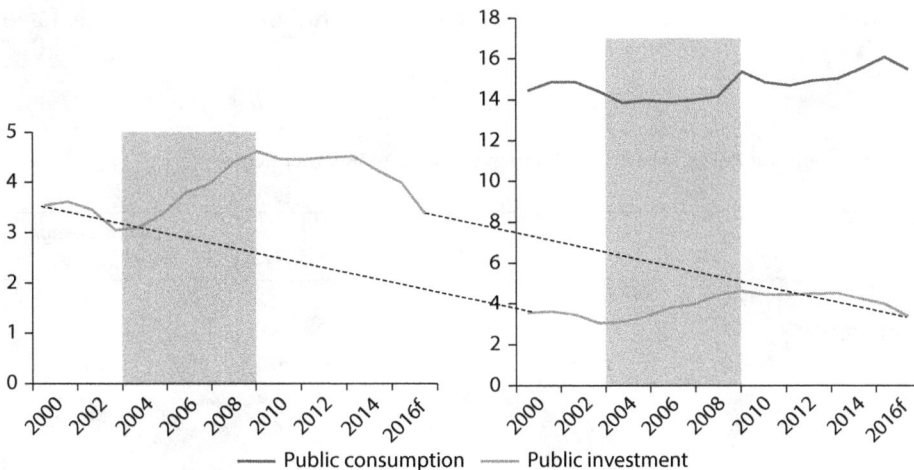

——— Public consumption ——— Public investment

Sources: World Development Indicators (http://data.worldbank.org/data-catalog/world-development-indicators); IMF World Economic Outlook database (https://www.imf.org/external/pubs/ft/weo/2017/01/weodata/index.aspx).
Note: Green shaded area represents the boom years of 2004–08. Regional average is weighed by GDP shares. GDP = gross domestic product.

consumption has remained many multiples of public investment, which hovered around a modest 3.0–4.5 percent of GDP—significantly lower than among competitors and peers, especially Asian ones (table 2.4).

The implications for infrastructure investment are dire. Though PPPs have played an important role, they only represent about 40 percent of infrastructure investments in the region. Further, about one-third of PPP financing comes from public institutions (and about half of them rely on some type of government support, creating contingent liabilities on public coffers). In other words, public and private investments are complements rather than substitutes. Without vigorous effort on the public side, infrastructure investments in the region are unlikely to increase. In the absence of fiscal space, this vigorous effort would require reducing public consumption to create space for public investments—something that is unlikely given existing budget rigidities and the current recession—and/or substantially increasing public spending efficiency.

A "Bifurcated" Fiscal Panorama in LAC

A highly heterogeneous fiscal space picture has emerged in the region, largely driven by trade structure (de la Torre and others 2016). We can identify two broad groups: (1) South America, dominated by net commodity exporters, which are generally following China's ups and downs; and (2) the Mexico-Central America-Caribbean (MCC) group, where net commodity importers prevail, and which is generally following the U.S. cycle. As figure 2.3 panels a and b show, fiscal balances have deteriorated markedly in most of South America, but not so much for the average MCC country.

But even within these broad groups, there is some heterogeneity. Fiscal deterioration has varied among South American countries. Faster-growing economies, such as Chile, Colombia, Paraguay, and Peru have fared better fiscally than slower-growing ones, such as Argentina, Brazil, and Ecuador (figure 2.3 panels c and d). On the whole, South American countries have

Table 2.4 In Latin America, Total Public Investment Is Much Lower than in Other Regions
Percentage of GDP

Region	2000–03	2004–08	2009–13	2013–16	Period average (2000–16)
East Asia and Pacific	17.5	15.5	14.8	12.2	15.1
Middle East and North Africa	5.7	7.5	9.1	8.9	7.8
South Asia	6.0	7.3	7.1	6.0	6.7
Sub-Saharan Africa	5.3	5.2	5.7	5.6	5.4
Europe and Central Asia	2.8	4.1	4.3	4.2	3.9
Latin America and the Caribbean	3.4	3.7	4.5	4.0	3.9

Sources: World Development Indicators (http://data.worldbank.org/data-catalog/world-development-indicators); IMF World Economic Outlook database (https://www.imf.org/external/pubs/ft/weo/2017/01/weodata/index.aspx).
Note: Regional averages are weighted using PPP GDP. 2016 is forecast. GDP = gross domestic product; PPP = public-private partnership.

Figure 2.3 Latin America and the Caribbean: Fiscal Bifurcation
Percentage of GDP

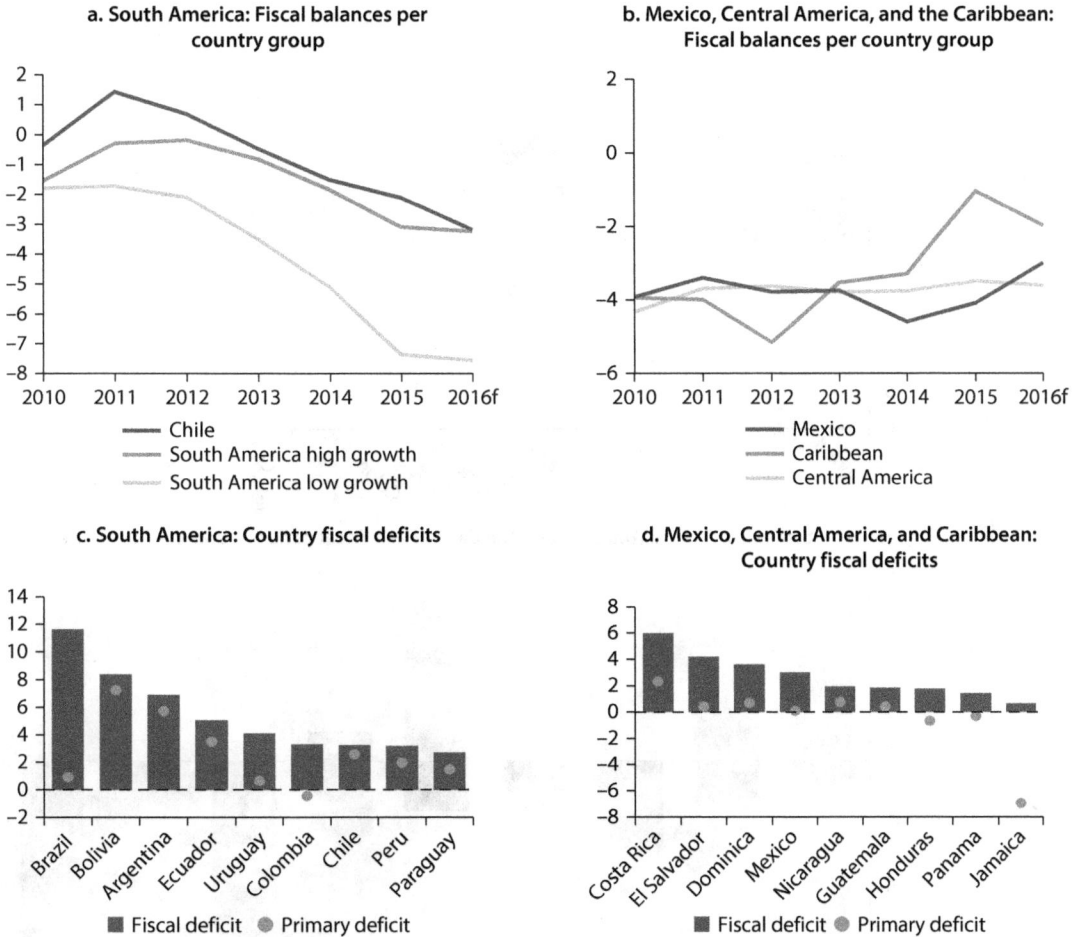

a. South America: Fiscal balances per country group

b. Mexico, Central America, and the Caribbean: Fiscal balances per country group

c. South America: Country fiscal deficits

d. Mexico, Central America, and Caribbean: Country fiscal deficits

Sources: IMF World Economic Outlook database (http://data.worldbank.org/data-catalog/world-development-indicators), and national sources. Prepared by the World Bank Latin America and the Caribbean Chief Economist Office.
Note: South America low growth includes Argentina, Brazil, and Ecuador; South America high growth includes Colombia, Peru, and Uruguay. Central America includes Costa Rica, El Salvador, and Guatemala; Caribbean includes the Dominican Republic, Haiti, and Jamaica.

not yet succeeded in their adjustment efforts: fiscal deficits have widened as expenditures continued to grow—with Ecuador a clear exception (figure 2.4, panel a). Other important differences exist among South American countries, attesting to the distinct nature of their fiscal woes: While interest payments play an outsize role in Brazil, Colombia, and Uruguay, primary expenditures are the dominant factor in Argentina, Bolivia, and República Bolivariana de Venezuela.

In contrast, there has not been a dramatic, widespread deterioration of fiscal balances in the MCC countries—even as they generally started from a weaker fiscal stance than their South American counterparts. Indeed, there has been

Figure 2.4 Latin America and the Caribbean: Sources of Changes in Fiscal Deficits

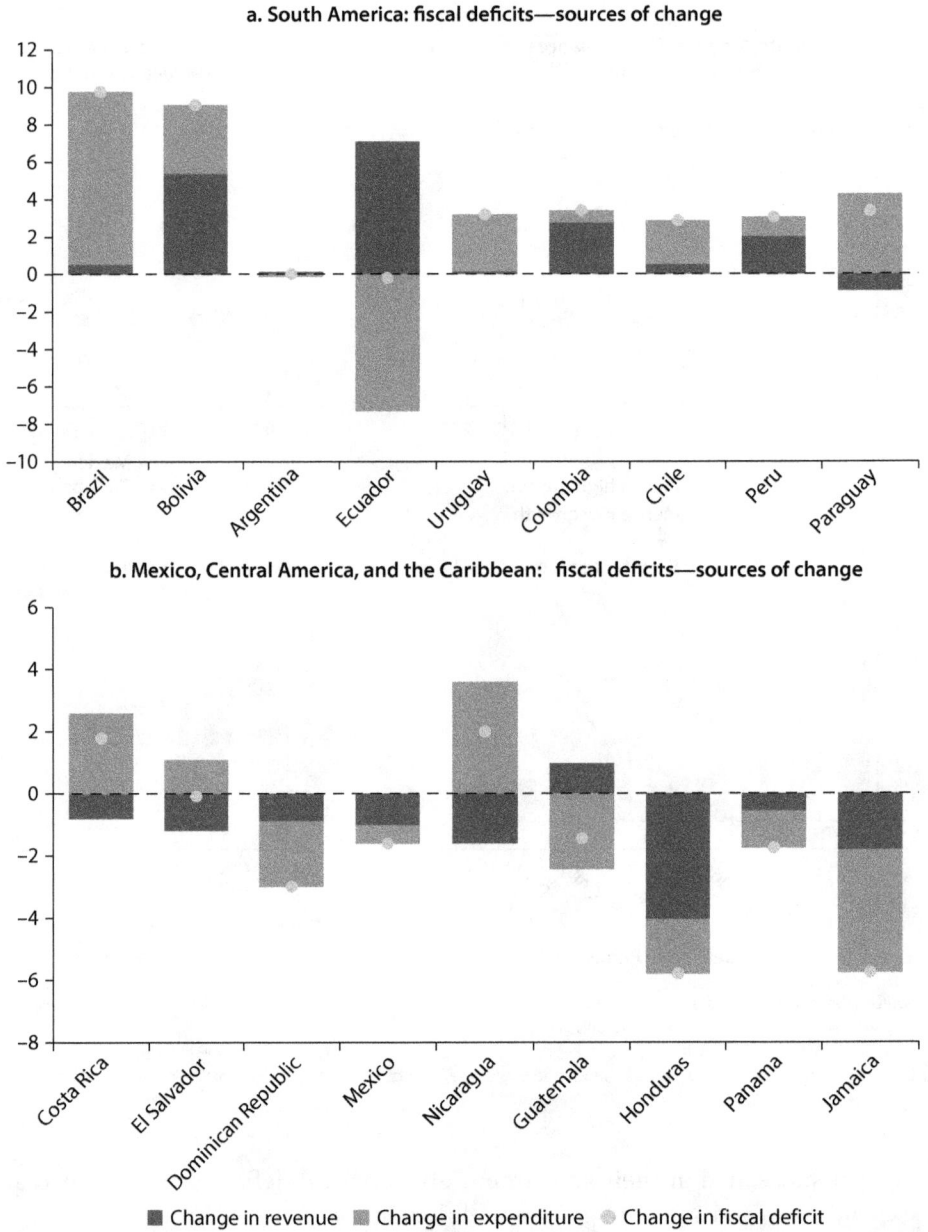

a. South America: fiscal deficits—sources of change

b. Mexico, Central America, and the Caribbean: fiscal deficits—sources of change

■ Change in revenue ■ Change in expenditure ● Change in fiscal deficit

Sources: IMF World Economic Outlook database (http://data.worldbank.org/data-catalog/world-development-indicators), and national sources. Prepared by the World Bank Latin America and the Caribbean Chief Economist Office.
Note: The changes are computed between the last observation and the point in time after 2009 when the lowest fiscal balance was recorded. If the lowest balance corresponds to the latest observation, the difference was computed with respect to the point in time when the fiscal balance was closest to zero. The values for the total and primary fiscal deficits correspond to the latest available observation.

some reduction in fiscal deficits, especially in the Caribbean (figure 2.4 panel b). Fiscal consolidation occurred mostly through expenditure reductions rather than through revenue increases. In the case of Jamaica, a massive reduction in its primary deficit was achieved, helping address the country's hitherto unsustainable debt trajectory. Nevertheless, in a few MCC countries (for example, Costa Rica and Nicaragua), the fiscal situation remains uncomfortable, characterized by high and increasing primary and/or overall fiscal deficits.

The *composition* of adjustment matters. It has been all too common in the past for countries to disproportionately cut capital expenditures as a more politically expedient way of adjusting. It is still not entirely clear whether current or capital spending is bearing the brunt of fiscal adjustment in the present round. Data coming out of recent IMF staff reports show a mixed picture. Capital spending as a share of GDP is projected to contract in Bolivia, Ecuador, and (to a lesser extent) Jamaica and Mexico, while remaining broadly stable in Costa Rica and Peru. More country-level information will be needed to ascertain clearly the composition of fiscal adjustment in the region—and its implications for public investments. The point remains, however, that few Latin American countries can boast of ample fiscal space with which to finance a significant infrastructure expansion.

Climate Change Is Creating New Challenges, but Possibly New Opportunities

Changing climatic conditions, natural disasters, and extreme weather events are affecting the ability of existing infrastructure to deliver services in Latin America. Melting glaciers and recurrent droughts are undermining hydroelectric production and may become a serious challenge for water-constrained cities. Storms, floods, and landslides wash away roads and bridges and destroy other infrastructure. Thus, infrastructure must become more resilient.

At the same time, Latin America has the world's cleanest energy matrix and plenty of potential to further reduce emissions associated with infrastructure—opportunities that carry local and immediate benefits such as reduced air pollution and congestion. This offers the region a potential competitive advantage, especially if carbon taxes are imposed in some of its key export markets. So infrastructure also needs to be made cleaner and more efficient.

Infrastructure Needs to Be More Resilient and Better Adapted to the Changing Climate

Disaster and climate risks are expected to increase in the region, with implications for infrastructure development (box 2.1). Energy, transport, and water and sanitation systems need to be built in more resilient ways to reduce disruptions during extreme events. In addition, climate change will alter the demand for infrastructure services: heat waves will increase electricity demand, droughts and

---

Box 2.1 How Will Climate Change Affect Latin America?

Latin America is exposed to many climate risks, most of which materialize through the water cycle. These risks vary by subregion but also depend on climate change. Impacts are expected to increase in intensity and severity as global temperatures continue to rise.

- *Most dry regions could get drier and most wet regions could get wetter.* Increased rainfall in tropical and subtropical Pacific coastlines and southern Brazil is in contrast with decreased precipitation in the Caribbean, Central America, northeast and central Brazil, and Patagonia. Rainfall could decrease 20–40 percent if global warming increases 4°C above preindustrial temperatures (a "4°C world").
- *Seasonal distribution of stream flows could become more variable.* Glaciers could disappear in a 4°C scenario and suffer considerable loss in a 2°C scenario. This retreat could cause glacial lake outbursts and flooding, as well as reduced water runoff in some river basins.
- *Increased risks of droughts and extreme heat could undermine seasonal water availability.* Higher mean temperatures and increased rainfall variability could extend dry spells and drought conditions by up to 20 percent in a 4°C scenario.
- *More intense rainfalls could increase the risks of landslides.* Excessive rainfall within short periods could overwhelm urban natural drainage systems. Landslide risks are highest on sloping terrain—where poor people often live.
- *The intensity and frequency of tropical storms will likely increase.* The frequency of the strongest tropical cyclones could increase by 40 percent in a 2°C world and by 80 percent in a 4°C world. Storms could increase coastal flooding, mostly in the Caribbean.
- *Higher sea levels could cause coastal flooding and erosion.* Projections vary by zone and range from an average of 0.38 meters in a 2°C world to 1.14 meters in a 4°C world. Such extreme coastal flooding and rising sea levels could expose many zones to the risk of storm surges.

Some of these risks will be conditioned by changes in ecosystems and feedback relationships. A 40 percent decrease in the Amazon's forest area could be a potential tipping point at which forest-climate interactions could decrease precipitation. Forest cover loss is already associated with droughts in the Amazon.

Sources: Magrin and others 2014; World Bank 2014c.

---

extreme rains will create the need for more water storage capacity, and increased flood risks will demand infrastructure solutions such as protective dams.

Extreme events already cause extensive damage to infrastructure. Rapid loss and damage assessments done after natural disasters in Latin America suggest that infrastructure bears a disproportionate share of the costs. The transport sector, in particular, bears a heavy burden (figure 2.5).

Climate change can interact with infrastructure in many different ways including the following (Magrin and others 2014; World Bank 2014c):

- *Extreme events such as intense rainfalls and storms are already damaging transport systems and causing widespread disruptions.* Intense rainfalls can cause flash floods and landslides, which can destroy bridges and other critical road

Figure 2.5 Disaster Damages for Infrastructure Are Highest for Transport
Percentage of total damage

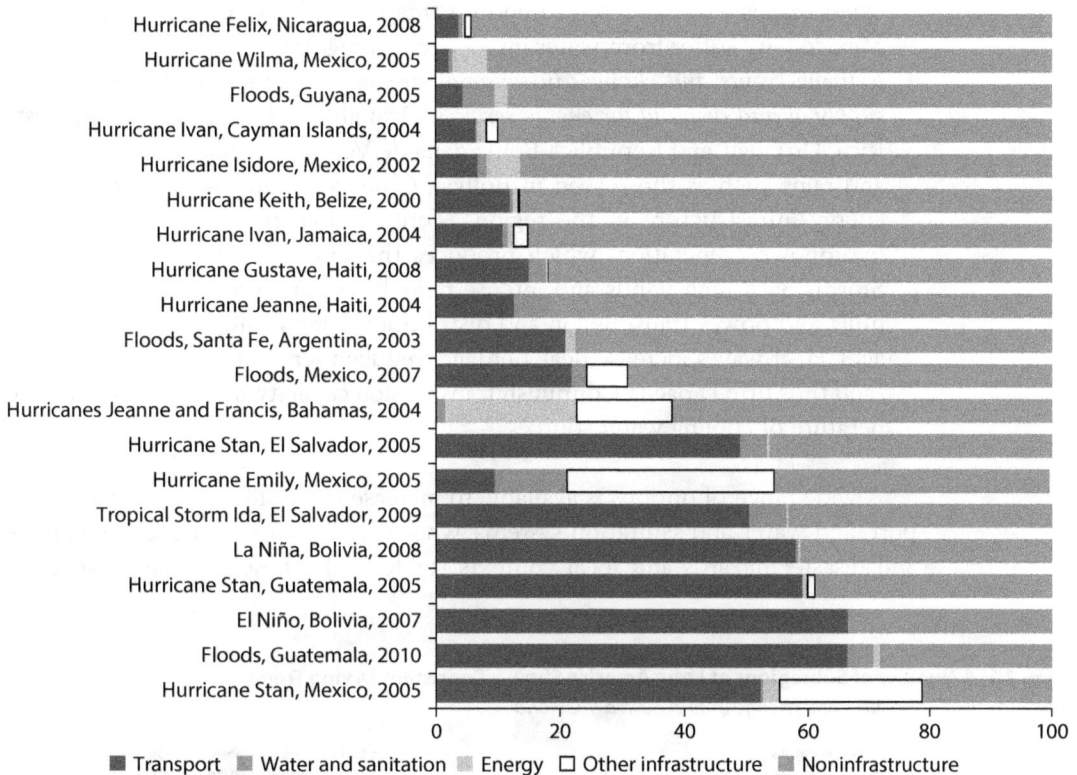

Source: GFDRR Loss and damage database (http://www.gfdrr.org/damageandlosses), accessed November 2016.

segments—leading to high repair costs and severe travel disruptions. In coastal cities and on Caribbean islands, where most critical transport systems are in low-lying areas, these impacts could be especially large. More intense tropical cyclones in combination with rising sea levels could extend port downtimes for ships, raising shipping costs and reducing trade.

• *Rising sea levels and intense El Niño events could threaten coastal infrastructure.* Combined with tropical storms, these could mean that a 100-year flood event formerly reaching 2.8 meters could reach nearly 8.0 meters by midcentury. This is a major concern given that 42,600 square kilometers containing more than 7.5 million inhabitants, and built capital valued at US$334 billion are situated at elevations below today's 100-year extreme sea level (Reguero and others 2015).

• *Rainfall variability and prolonged water stress could threaten water supply in parts of the region.* Although Latin America has relatively abundant water resources, the spatial and temporal dimensions of water vary (Miralles-Wilhelm 2016). Notwithstanding large uncertainties, areas in the Amazon basin, northern Mexico, northeast Brazil, the Pacific coasts of Chile and Peru, and countries in the Caribbean and Central America show a consistent drying trend that is also expected to endure (map 2.1). Large cities like Lima and Mexico City suffer from water insecurity and regular water shortages.

- *Extreme events and changes in seasonal stream flows are already changing the supply of and demand for energy services.* Droughts in Brazil, Colombia, Costa Rica, Uruguay, and República Bolivariana de Venezuela, and torrential storms and rains such as those seen in Bolivia, Chile, and Paraguay are threatening energy infrastructure in the region. More variable river runoff could limit hydropower generation, which produces the most electricity in the region. Storms with high winds and intense rainfalls could damage pipelines, windmills, and power transmission and distribution lines, resulting in power shortages. Heat waves increase peak demand, reduce thermal conversion efficiency (and thus firm capacity), diminish transmission capacity, and increase the temperature of cooling water sources.

A wide range of options is available to increase the resilience of energy, transport, and water and sanitation systems, whose effectiveness depends on climate and disaster hazards and local contexts (table 2.5). These include engineering

Map 2.1 A Number of Subregions of Latin America Show a Consistent Drying Trend
Water availability in 2015 and change until 2050 in a 4°C world

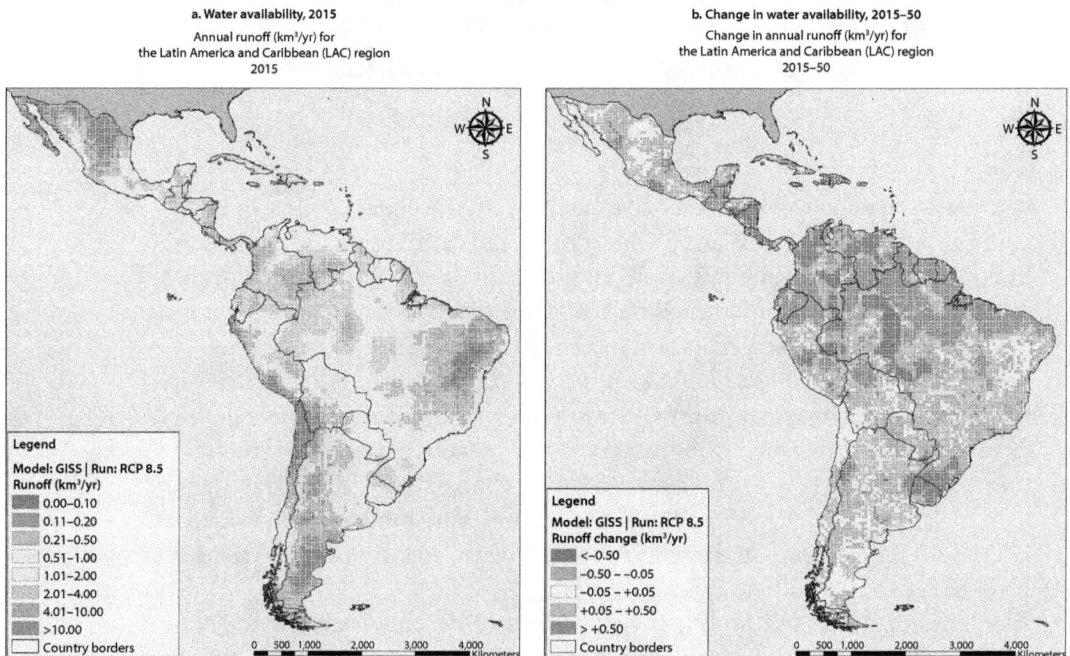

a. Water availability, 2015
Annual runoff (km³/yr) for
the Latin America and Caribbean (LAC) region
2015

Legend
Model: GISS | Run: RCP 8.5
Runoff (km³/yr)
- 0.00–0.10
- 0.11–0.20
- 0.21–0.50
- 0.51–1.00
- 1.01–2.00
- 2.01–4.00
- 4.01–10.00
- >10.00
- Country borders

0 500 1,000   2,000   3,000   4,000
Kilometers

b. Change in water availability, 2015–50
Change in annual runoff (km³/yr) for
the Latin America and Caribbean (LAC) region
2015–50

Legend
Model: GISS | Run: RCP 8.5
Runoff change (km³/yr)
- <−0.50
- −0.50 – −0.05
- −0.05 – +0.05
- +0.05 – +0.50
- > +0.50
- Country borders

0 500 1,000   2,000   3,000   4,000
Kilometers

Source: Miralles-Wilhelm 2016.
Note: Projections for 2050 are for a world on a trajectory to reach 4°C warming by 2100.

Table 2.5 Ways to Make Infrastructure More Resilient, by Approach and Sector

Approach	Electricity	Transport	Water and sanitation
Engineering	• Adjusted design codes for power plants and electricity grids • Underground cable networks • Increased system capacity • Increased grid integration	• Hazard-resistant construction standards and design parameters for roads and bridges • Strengthened/heightened protection walls for roads • Raised height of causeway roads in ports	• More or better-maintained water reservoirs and storage • Pumping stations • Sewerage work • Drainage systems
Technological	• Renewable technologies	• Use of new designs and materials • Use of information technologies to control traffic	• Water-saving technologies • Hydrometeorological monitoring • Desalination technologies
Ecosystem based	• Water flow regulation and sediment control through watershed protection	• Slope stabilization through replanting	• Protection of upstream areas that provide water regulation and filtration
Institutional	• Hazard mapping, vulnerability assessments, spatial planning, disaster preparedness, and contingency plans		

Source: Adapted from IPCC 2014.

options (to retrofit existing infrastructure or design new infrastructure), technological and ecosystem-based options (such as protecting systems through conservation or restoration of natural systems), and institutional actions (such as rerouting of roads and electricity grids, reducing exposure to hazards).

Given the long lifespan of most infrastructure, robust design options and adaptive pathways that build in flexibility are needed to manage future uncertainties (box 2.2). Although resilience planning is still a nascent field—especially in the transport and electricity sectors—there is growing recognition that uncertainties about future climate impacts need to be incorporated in today's investment decisions. A recent analysis by the World Bank and SEDAPAL, Lima's water utility, did just that and developed a robust investment strategy that ensures water reliability across as wide a range of future conditions as possible (Kalra and others 2015). Other key water utilities in the region—such as Aguas de Manizales in Colombia and Empresa Pública Metropolitana de Alcantarillado y Agua Potable de Quito in Ecuador—have also conducted comprehensive risk studies to prepare for extreme events (Balcázar 2012).

Resilient strategies need not necessarily cost more. The resilient investment plan developed by Lima's water utility (box 2.2) resulted in changed rather than more investment, which should reduce investment costs by 25 percent, thanks to an increased emphasis on demand-side management, and a focus on "no-regret" investments (Kalra and others 2015).

But estimating an overall cost of adapting to climate change is made difficult, if not impossible, by the fact that adaptation costs are highly situation and site specific. Not surprisingly then, available estimates vary greatly along with the cost elements and climate scenarios considered. One study estimated that for

Brazil alone, some US$50 billion of capital investments would be needed to ensure reliable electricity supply by 2035 because of the projected lack of reliability of hydroelectricity (de Lucena, Schaeffer, and Szklo 2010). Background work for this report suggests that providing additional reservoir capacity to meet future industrial and municipal water demand across Latin America could cost US$44 billion to US$57 billion between now and 2050—an annual average of US$1.3 billion to US$1.6 billion (Miralles-Wilhelm 2016), higher than the previous estimate of US$1 billion a year (Ward and others 2010). The World Bank's *Economics of Adaptation to Climate Change* estimated that the total costs of adapting infrastructure in Latin America could be around US$4 billion a year (World Bank 2010).[4]

But given the avoided costs from negative impacts, investing in more robust infrastructure can have a high payoff. A study of Peru's 2007 earthquake estimates that the country could have saved 27 times the reconditioning spent on water and sanitation infrastructure if the affected systems had had proper maintenance and been built using earthquake-resistant materials (Cannock and others 2011). Also in Peru, the benefits of making critical segments of the country's road network flood resilient exceed the costs in almost all future

---

Box 2.2 Nonprobabilistic Decision Making under Uncertainty Methodologies

Although the scientific evidence for a changing climate is clear, uncertainty about the speed and intensity of these changes is high. In this context, it is impossible to define probabilities for future climate conditions or extreme climatic events.

To account for these deep uncertainties, nonprobabilistic approaches are needed—often called decision making under uncertainty (DMU) methodologies. Rather than weighting futures probabilistically to define an optimal strategy, these methods seek to identify robust strategies—those that satisfy decision makers' objectives in many plausible futures (Kalra and others 2014; Lempert and others 2013). These methods have been applied, for example, to define a robust portfolio of water reservoirs for implementing Lima's long-term water resource plan (Kalra and others 2015). The basic steps include identifying all the possible conditions that could make a project fail and deciding whether these are reasonable scenarios to try and protect against based on decision makers' tolerance for risk, inputs from experts and stakeholders on whether the scenarios are worth worrying about, and the costs of robust options.

Such an approach can also help to define pathways that allow for flexibility and adjustment of the strategy once new information becomes available and future developments become more predictable. For example, for Lima, an adaptive portfolio of water reservoirs was identified, starting with no-regret reservoirs to be implemented in the near term (figure B2.2.1). In the medium term, reservoirs can be added depending on the feasibility of and need for more complicated projects. In the long term, decision makers can choose the reservoir combinations that meet future water demand.

box continues next page

Box 2.2 Nonprobabilistic Decision Making under Uncertainty Methodologies (continued)

Figure B2.2.1 Robust and Adaptive Portfolio of Water Reservoirs to Implement Lima's Water Resource Master Plan

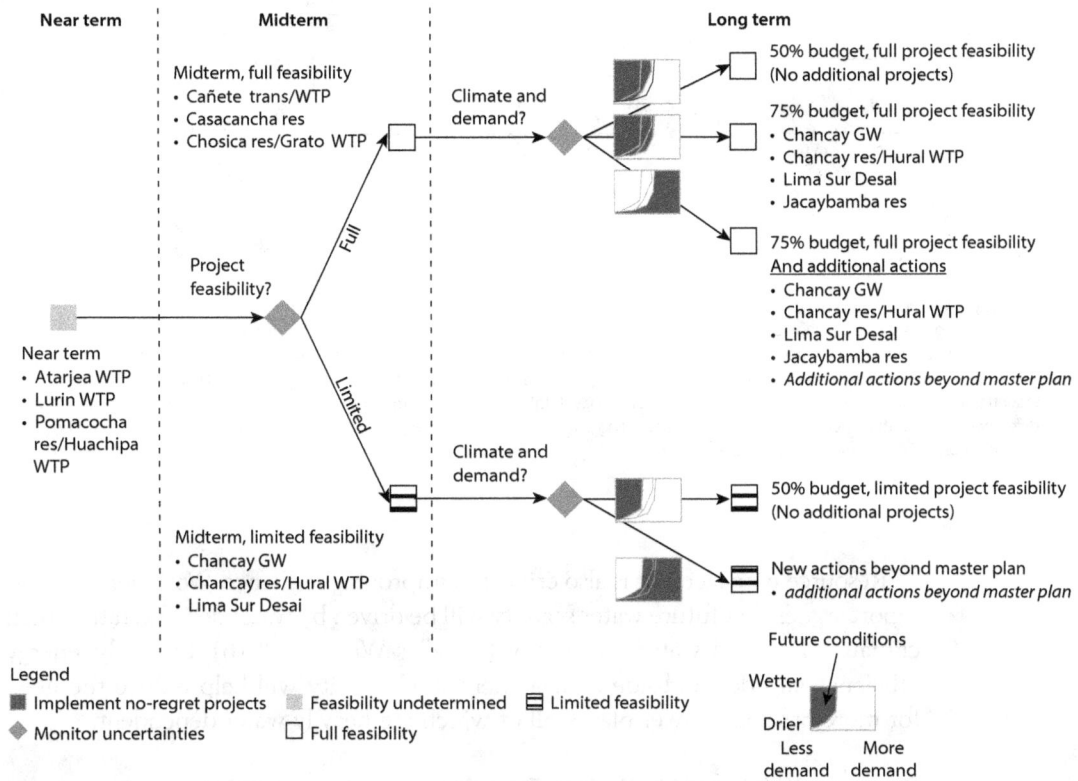

Source: Kalra and others 2015.
Note: Desal = desalinization plant; GW = groundwater; Res = reservoir; WTP = water treatment plant.

scenarios (figure 2.6). Generally, however, benefits—like costs—are very location specific and very difficult to estimate.

Cross-sectoral coordination mechanisms and integrated planning frameworks help make infrastructure sectors more prepared and responsive. Effective solutions need to work across sectors and levels of governments to align local plans with regional and national strategies. For example, after Chile's 2010 earthquake, the biggest challenge for water and sanitation systems was the absence of electricity. Chile's experience shows that in addition to improving the response capacity of individual water utilities, these utilities need to be integrated in a regional, multisector contingency plan (Peña and others 2012). Recent droughts in São Paulo have shown the need not only for technological solutions, but also for assigning water rights in basins shared among jurisdictions (Peña and others 2015).

Figure 2.6 Flood Proofing Critical Road Segments in Peru Pays Off in Almost All Possible Scenarios

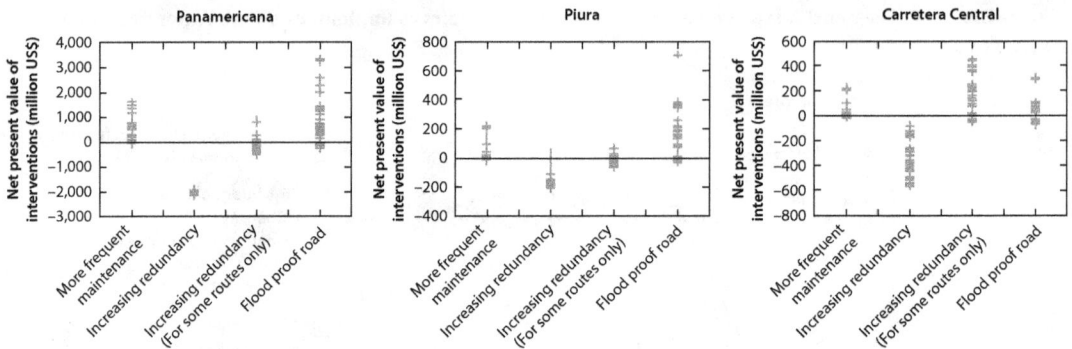

Source: Briceño-Garmendia, Moroz, and Rozenberg 2015.
Note: The three figures show for critical segments of three major roads in Peru (Panamericana, Piura, and Carretera Central) the net present value of four possible interventions: more frequent maintenance, increasing redundancy (for all or just some routes), and flood proofing. The net present value of these interventions is estimated for hundreds of possible scenarios—depicted in the many horizontal bars—that explore uncertainties around possible future flooding, damage associated with this flooding, and time to rebuild. The net present value is calculated as the difference between the reduction in annual losses (including user costs and rehabilitation costs) due to intervention and the investment and maintenance costs of the intervention option.

Resource management is also critical to improving resilience. Work done for this report argues that future water scarcity will be driven by water demand rather than climate-influenced water availability (Miralles-Wilhelm 2016). Similarly, energy efficiency and demand-side management in electricity will help reduce the need for more baseload power plants, all of which are heavily water dependent.

Pressures Will Mount to Reduce Emissions from Infrastructure

Infrastructure-related sectors will play an important role in achieving Latin America's emission targets. Although the region accounts for just 11 percent of global emissions, significant emission reductions are needed to remain within the global 2°C warming target. Emissions in Latin America grew from 3.6 gigatons of carbon dioxide equivalent ($GtCO_2e$) in 1990 to 4.4 $GtCO_2e$ in 2012, with a doubling of emissions from electricity and transport and a 50 percent increase in "other energy," more than offsetting an 18 percent decrease in emissions from land-use changes and forestry (figure 2.7).

Among energy-related sectors, transport is the fastest growing contributor to emissions (figure 2.7). It is also a larger-than-average contributor: in 2012, transport accounted for 32 percent (compared with 23 percent globally) of energy-related emissions. Most Latin American countries saw rapid increases in emissions from both electricity and transport: in Brazil, both shot up more than 60 percent, while in Peru, emissions from electricity generation tripled and emissions from transport grew 80 percent (figure 2.8).

Without action, emissions from infrastructure-related sectors are likely to increase further. According to the Global Energy Assessment (GEA) model developed by the International Institute for Applied Systems Analysis, a

Figure 2.7 Latin America's Greenhouse Gas Emissions Have Been Growing, Driven by Energy-Related Emissions, 1990–2012

Gigatons of carbon dioxide equivalent (GtCO₂e)

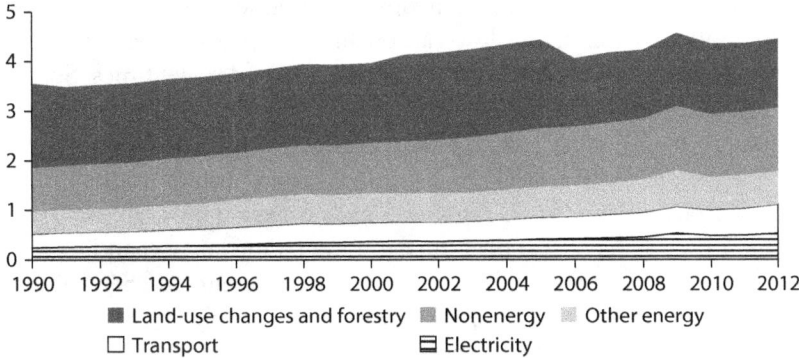

■ Land-use changes and forestry ▨ Nonenergy ▨ Other energy
□ Transport   ▤ Electricity

Source: WRI 2016.

Figure 2.8 Emissions from Energy-Related Sectors Have Been Growing since 2000

Megatons of carbon dioxide equivalent MtCO₂e

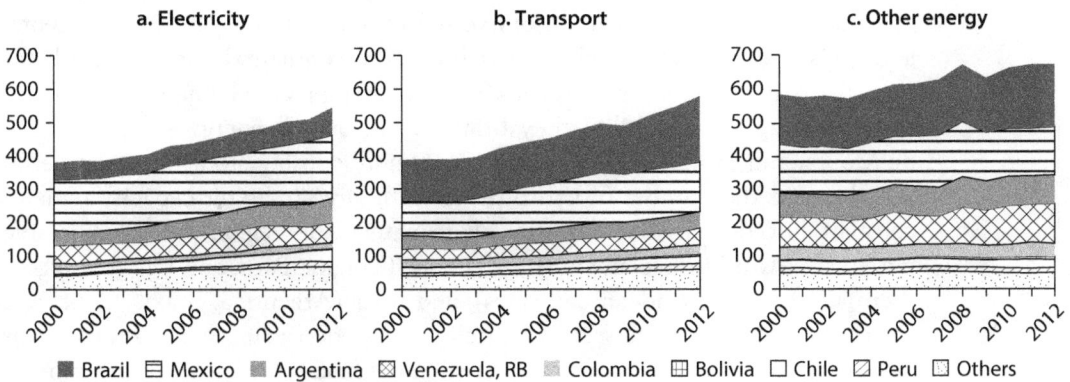

a. Electricity   b. Transport   c. Other energy

■ Brazil ▤ Mexico ▨ Argentina ⊠ Venezuela, RB ▨ Colombia ⊞ Bolivia □ Chile ▨ Peru □ Others

Source: WRI 2016.

business-as-usual scenario with increased motorization and decreased reliance on hydroelectricity would see energy-related emissions in the region more than double between 2010 and 2050 (Vergara and others 2013).

Mitigation options in energy-related sectors could reduce emissions considerably. Estimates from the GEA model suggest that energy-focused mitigation strategies in Latin America could cut annual emissions by up to 4.1 GtCO₂e by 2050, reducing energy-related emissions to almost zero. Such savings would require 60–80 percent of the primary energy mix to come from renewables, 75–100 percent of the electricity mix to come from low-carbon sources, and further improvements in energy intensity (Vergara and others 2013).

More generally, mitigation strategies involve action on three fronts: decarbonizing energy mixes, electrification (notably of transport), and increasing efficiency (Fay and others 2015).

In transport, the main mitigation options include shifting to lower-carbon transport modes, switching to low-carbon fuels, improving vehicle and engine performance, and reducing the number of journeys and travel times. Some of the greatest gains could come from developing bus rapid transit (BRT) systems. These systems have mainstreamed bus-based mass transit by offering high capacity and good service at relatively low costs and have been developed in cities in Argentina, Brazil, Ecuador, Guatemala, and Uruguay (World Bank 2013b). Important advances have also been made in upgrading and expanding rail-based systems, such as in the metropolitan areas of Rio de Janeiro and São Paulo. La Paz has developed a cable car to bring passengers from the suburbs to the city center. Given the relatively clean energy mix, switching to electric cars can reduce overall emissions, as shown in Bogota (Delgado and others 2014). Similarly, enhancing the quality and quantity of nonmotorized transport (such as cycling and walking) can cut emissions. For interregional or intercountry transport, the expansion of waterways, such as the Panama Canal, is another option for reducing emissions (de Marucci 2012).

Electricity decarbonization is possible through increased reliance on renewable energy. However, expansion of hydroelectricity is limited by environmental and social concerns and climatic variability. Environmental concerns push for run-of-the-river plants, which means existing reservoirs are being used in excess, compromising the flexibility they bring to the overall energy system (Broad, de Moura, and Howells 2016). Thus, the region is losing storage capacity each year, because the number of hydro plants with large reservoir capacity remains constant but demand is increasing. Fortunately, the region has considerable potential in wind (especially in Brazil, Chile, Ecuador, Peru, and Uruguay), geothermal (mostly in Andean countries), and solar (Argentina, Brazil, Chile, and Peru have areas for large-scale electricity production using concentrated solar power plants). Equally important, the region has made good progress on improving the business environment for investment in renewables—although it remains far from the good practice frontier, as demonstrated by the Readiness for Investment in Sustainable Energy Index (box 2.3).

The region has significant potential for improved energy efficiency—which is critical not just to reduce emissions but also to reduce investment needs and local pollution. Latin America's energy intensity is declining, but at a slower rate than in other regions (which, admittedly, have much more room for improvement) and not in all countries. Brazil has actually increased its energy intensity from 5.1 megajoules per 2010 US$ in 1990 to 5.3 in 2012. Significant scope for further reducing energy intensity exists in transport, agriculture, industry, and commercial services. But significant improvements in regulations and policies—as well as their implementation—are needed (box 2.3).

The question is whether Latin America's power sector is ready for the kind of transformation and new business models that are emerging in advanced

---

Box 2.3 The Region Is Improving Its Business Environment for Renewable Energy Investments, although It Remains Far from the Good Practice Frontier

The Readiness for Investment in Sustainable Energy Index (RISE)—a suite of indicators that assesses the legal and regulatory environment for investment in sustainable energy, including renewable energy, energy efficiency, and energy access—gives Latin America a 52 percent score ("average/to be improved") for renewable energy and 41 percent for energy efficiency. This score is better than Sub-Saharan Africa's score but below other developing regions, especially for energy efficiency. The index evaluates whether a region has introduced key measures on planning, policies and regulation, and administrative efficiency, and assesses counterparty risk and the existence of carbon pricing and monitoring.

In its first global rollout (2015), RISE covered 14 Latin American countries: Argentina, Bolivia, Brazil, Chile, Colombia, the Dominican Republic, Ecuador, Guatemala, Haiti, Honduras, Mexico, Nicaragua, Peru, and República Bolivariana de Venezuela. Most of these countries have introduced laws, regulations, targets, and action plans to promote renewable energy development (Haiti and República Bolivariana de Venezuela are exceptions). Most have also developed resource mappings and integrated renewable energy into traditional expansion planning. But it is in the details of regulations, operational rules, and planning where countries still need progress. For example, few countries in the region consider renewable energy scale-up in their transmission planning, and few produce strategic plans or provide zoning guidance on siting, which is essential to investors.

Most countries also need to make regulatory and policy incentives more efficient and effective and improve the creditworthiness of their utilities to make them more attractive to potential investors. Finally, credit enhancement and risk-mitigation instruments—such as letters of credit, escrow accounts, and payment guarantees—are needed to attract private investment in renewable energy, but few governments in the sample are able to offer such incentives.

A few countries in the region have developed policies, regulations, and institutions to boost energy efficiency (Mexico, and to a lesser extent Brazil and Colombia). But implementation has been weak, and most has occurred in the context of crises and deficits in energy supplies. In addition, fossil fuel subsidies remain high in countries such as Argentina, Bolivia, Chile, Ecuador, and República Bolivariana de Venezuela.

Sources: Banerjee and others 2017; World Bank, forthcoming a.

---

economies as a result of a number of related disruptive factors: new technologies and changing cost curves, climate change pressures (for both mitigation and adaptation), shifts in demand profiles associated with distributed generation (the consumer as producer—or prosumer), increased demand for air conditioning and cooling, and possibly demand for electric transportation (table 2.6).

According to recent World Bank analysis, Latin America is reasonably well positioned to transform its energy sector and leapfrog to new business models (World Bank, forthcoming a). Successful reforms in the 1990s in several

Table 2.6 Latin America's Disruptive Challenges in the Power Sector

Challenge	Response
Greening the grid and transportation • Expand nonconventional renewables sustainably—both at utility scale and distributed generation. • Expand clean mass transport solutions and increase market penetration of energy-efficient vehicles (cars, trucks, buses).	• The region already has the world's greenest energy matrix. It makes extensive use of hydro resources and modest use of coal, although coal remains the dominant fuel for power generation in Mexico and smaller markets. • Most countries are deploying grid-connected nonconventional renewables, pioneering the use of competitive schemes (auctions). Penetration of distributed generation is still modest. • Large cities are adopting simple mass transit solutions (such as bus rapid transit corridors). • Vehicular compressed natural gas (CNG), blended gas, and fuel ethanol have significantly reduced CO_2 and other pollution emissions.
Making the power system more resilient • Increase automation and technical resilience of the grid (supply side). • Foster the adoption of decentralized solutions. • Develop a comprehensive load-control and demand-response program, particularly in load-congested areas. • Combine storage (thermal, electric) with load control to mitigate renewable intermittency.	• Distribution automation has helped make the grid more resilient with fault location, automated crew dispatch, and other ways to handle catastrophic events. • The combination of complementary nonconventional renewables with hydro storage has made the system more resilient to drought and helped manage intermittency cost effectively. • Much more is needed on demand-side management, including stronger interface with clients, energy management initiatives, and demand response. There have been a few cases of effective power crisis management using demand response (Argentina, Brazil, Chile, Colombia, Panama), but it has not been embedded in the regulatory compact.
New utility model and regulatory compact • Increase the role of the utility (or supplier) in going "beyond the meter" in supporting energy efficiency and distributed generation. • Create specific policy directives to foster energy efficiency, demand-side management, and renewable energy initiatives. • Create specific regulations to encourage utilities to engage beyond the meter, such as decoupling, and shared savings.	• Unlike in Europe, the Republic of Korea, and the United States, utilities are not yet a key vehicle for delivering energy efficiency and demand-side management, even though they are the most effective channel for achieving significant energy and demand reduction. Only Brazil has a "wire charge" of 1 percent of utility revenue, half of which is dedicated to energy efficiency. This is largely due to inadequate regulations, which do not compensate the utility for energy efficiency efforts.
Creative business and financial models • New players and applications are emerging in collaboration or competition with the utility in providing information, load control, home management systems, and distributed generation. • New value-added services and players are emerging—such as district cooling facilities, energy service companies, and concessions for street lighting. • New financial models and products are on the market to manage a range of new and old risks.	• Power sector in the region is still dominated by regulated utilities and independent producers. In industrial countries, there are a multitude of other players (marketers, demand aggregators, curtailment service providers, home management systems, and others) working in collaboration or in competition with utilities, and they facilitate the diffusion and adoption of technologies for which the traditional utility has no appetite or interest. • A few forward-looking utilities have established unregulated subsidiaries to provide value-added services, such as Light ESCO (energy services in Rio) and EPM (district cooling in Medellín). • The power sector lacks financial instruments to deal with a variety of new risks, particularly on the climate front. Some interesting solutions have emerged in Uruguay (low-hydrology hedge instrument) and Colombia (auctioned *Cargo por Confiabilidad*).

Source: World Bank, forthcoming a.

medium-size and large countries show that the region's power sector can embrace and manage change. The region has some of the most sophisticated power sectors among developing regions and is largely prepared to confront some of the challenges facing 21st-century utilities. For example, Latin America pioneered the use of competitive procurement for renewables, significantly and sustainably scaling up wind and solar generation.

These new technologies and a potential transformation of the business model could mean that the clean way forward is the cheapest. Modeling done for this report finds that South America would need to invest US$23 billion to US$24 billion a year in additional generation capacity under a business-as-usual scenario or even under the nationally determined contributions (NDCs) that countries in the region offered at the 2016 Paris Climate Conference (COP21) (table 2.7). But under a disruption scenario that compares with the NDCs in terms of large-scale renewable energy but makes much greater use of new technology for smart grids, decentralized generation, and energy efficiency by both grids and end users, costs could drop to US$8.4 billion a year between now and 2031. Leapfrogging, perhaps not surprisingly, could save the region a lot of money.

But a number of issues would need to be tackled for this transformation to happen. Most utilities in the region lack the skills to interact with customers more actively—a challenge given the role that utilities must play in implementing integrated planning, fostering energy efficiency, helping clients manage load, and working with end users to scale up distributed generation. Further, the transformation needed will be driven by changes in policies and regulations. Policy makers will need to develop national energy goals and policy tools, while regulators must provide utilities with incentives to engage "beyond the meter"—moving away from pure concepts of "return on assets" and

Table 2.7 The Costs of a Green Transition Could Drop Dramatically in South America if Full Use Is Made of New Technologies and Business Models

Model and scenarios	Investment (US$ billion)	Additional capacity/year (gigawatts)	Investment/year (US$ billion)
SAMBA (From 2018 to 2031)			
• Business as usual	303.0	9.1	23.3
• RET	336.5	101.2	25.9
• INDC	310.1	9.2	23.9
• Disruption	109.2	3.1	8.4
ICEPAC SA BAU (From 2012 to 2031)			
• Business as usual	315.9	7.77	24.3

Source: Broad, de Moura, and Howells 2016; World Bank, forthcoming a.
Note: SAMBA is the South America Electricity model developed by KTH Divisions of Systems Analysis. RET is a scenario with higher levels of renewable penetration but rapid growth in demand; INDC includes all renewable additions envisaged under countries' Intended Nationally Determined Contributions as per the UNFCCC Paris Agreement; Disruption includes the same large-scale renewable energy as under the NDCs but much greater decentralized renewable energy and energy efficiency, along with smart grids. ICEPAC is based on national expansion plans and demand estimates (OLADE's Super Model). Note that for ease of comparison, SAMBA prices were applied to the capacity expansion of ICEPAC (ICEPAC assumes much lower prices).

"revenues coupled to sales" to a new approach that compensates utilities for a broader set of services provided to clients.

More generally, and beyond the electricity sector, long-term planning is critical to greening the region's infrastructure. The optimal strategy and mix of abatement options depend on the time horizon and end goal. An example from Brazil shows how the planning horizon will affect what the "right" strategy looks like (figure 2.9). A strategy for 2020 makes more use of measures that are cheap and quick to implement, such as new processes and improvements in refineries. Measures for 2030 are costlier but have much larger abatement potential in the long term, such as building a new metro system. When designing an emissions reduction plan, costs, time to implement, and overall emissions reduction potential all need to be considered. Options in transport that take time to reach their full potential, but are required to reach long-term goals, need to get started early.

Urbanization and Changing Socioeconomics Are Complicating Matters

Latin America is highly urban, yet its cities are still seeing growth and transformation, with infrastructure both leading and following these changes.[5] Urbanization has been one of the drivers of increased access to infrastructure services, making it easier to achieve economies of scale. But these savings depend on the density of cities: encouraging compact development instead of sprawl can reduce public infrastructure and service costs by 10–40 percent (Litman 2015; Marulanda and others 2015). There is a limit to the gains from densification, however, as the limits of bulk infrastructure can be reached above a certain threshold of density (Libertun de Guren and Guerrero Compéan 2016).

Figure 2.9 In Brazil, Long-Term Planning Shifts Optimal Abatement Strategies
Emission reduction by 2020, megatons of carbon dioxide (MtCO$_2$)

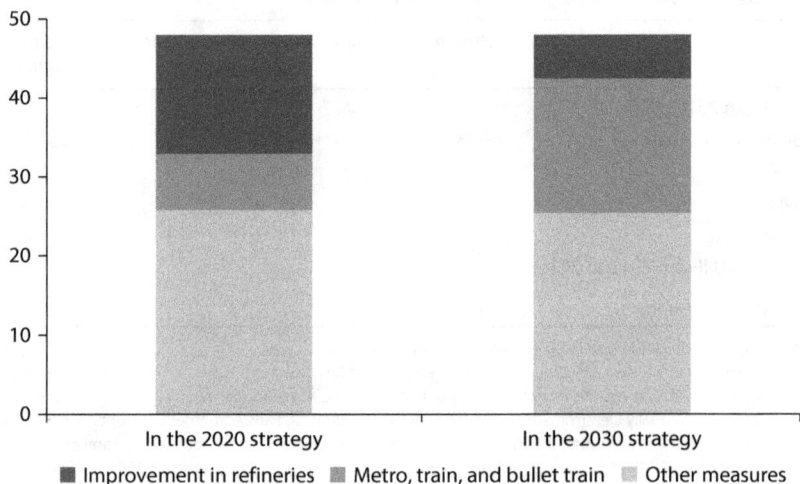

Source: Vogt-Schilb, Hallegatte, and de Gouvello 2015.

But housing, urban, and infrastructure policies are encouraging Latin America cities to expand at the periphery, with serious implications for infrastructure service costs. The region's built-up areas have expanded rapidly in recent decades. If expansion patterns continue unchanged, built-up urban areas will double in the region by 2035. Density has declined in Brasilia, Buenos Aires, La Paz, Montevideo, and Santiago. This increase in sprawl is largely policy driven: in Buenos Aires, for example, transport, land use, and housing policies are driving factors of low density growth in the periphery (Inostroza, Baur, and Csaplovics 2010). And while in Mexico only 14 percent of cities over 100,000 inhabitants "sprawled" between 1990 and 2010, most still have relatively low population densities, with immediate implications for infrastructure investment needs. The World Bank's Mexico Urbanization Review found that denser urbanization would reduce infrastructure investment and maintenance costs by 41 percent in Merida and 67 percent in Los Cabos compared to business-as-usual urbanization (Kim and Zangerling 2016).

In addition, some 25 percent of Latin America's city dwellers are believed to be living in slums (UN-Habitat 2013), many in areas not suitable for residential construction. Slums are often located in flood-prone or environmentally protected areas that put slum dwellers at high risk of natural disasters or create hazards for others (for example, when slums are in areas that threaten urban watersheds, as in Curitiba). Combined with disorderly and dense occupation that hinders work on access roads or water, sewerage, or drainage work, this complicates infrastructure provision and raises the costs. As a result, estimates are that upgrading a slum costs two to eight times more than regular land development (Abiko and others 2007). The implications are serious for infrastructure investment costs given that infrastructure typically represents some 70 percent of slum upgrading costs (Marulanda and others 2015).

What about changing socioeconomics? Latin America's middle class grew by about 50 percent during the boom years of 2003–09 (Ferreira and others 2012) reaching about 30 percent of the population just as the share of the population living in poverty fell by an equivalent amount. The vast majority of this middle class, as well as those approaching middle-class status, have access to electricity. Most also have access to water, while relatively few have access to sanitation (figure 2.10). Most reside in urban areas where they presumably have access to paved roads and some type of public transportation.

But this growing middle and near-middle class is far from being a saturated market in terms of consumer durables. A small share of the upper income deciles own the full suite of consumer durables (refrigerators, washing machines, air conditioners, computers, cars) that characterize the middle classes in high-income countries and drives their energy consumption and demand for infrastructure services: on average, some 90 percent own refrigerators, though that share drops rapidly with other durables (70–80 percent for washing machines, and 40 percent for cars) and for the near-middle class decile (figure 2.11).

Potentially facilitating access to durables is the boom in consumer credit that occurred in the last decade in Latin America, increasing from 9 percent

Figure 2.10 Good, Bad, and Worst: Almost All but the Poorest Consumers in Latin America Have Access to Electricity; Access to Water Is Less Universal; Access to Sanitation is Low, Even among the Middle Class

Percentage of population decile

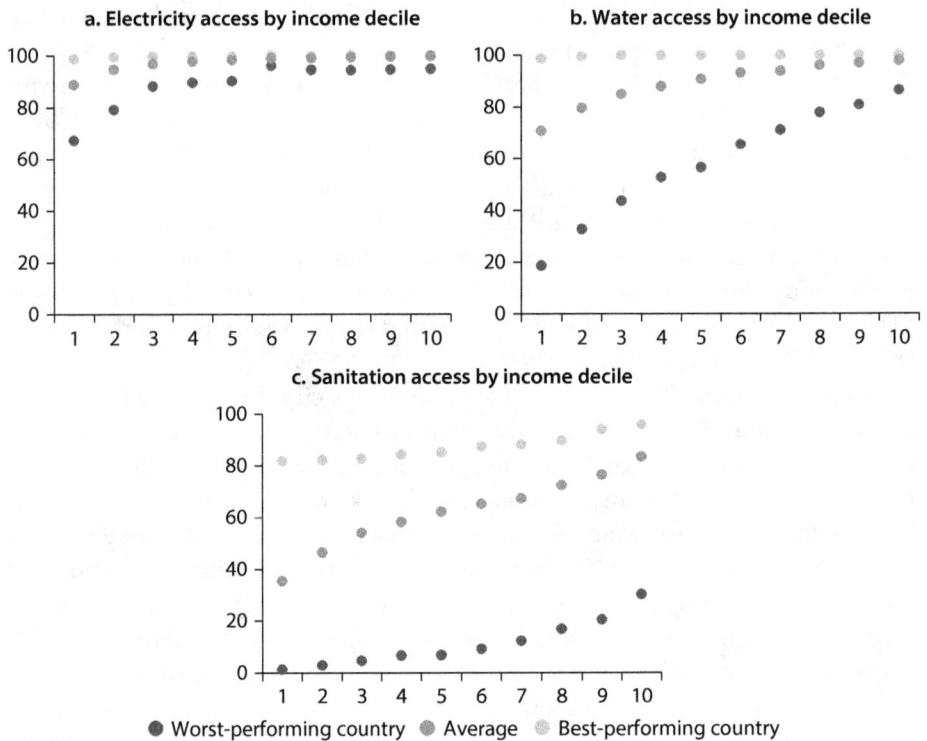

a. Electricity access by income decile

b. Water access by income decile

c. Sanitation access by income decile

● Worst-performing country ● Average ● Best-performing country

Source: Fay and Straub 2016.

Note: Deciles are defined region wide, so the figure shows how Latin Americans earning similar incomes (within a decile) may experience wide variation in access to services, depending on the country where they live. For example, the average rate of access to water among households in Latin America's poorest decile varies from 20 percent in the worst-performing country to 100 percent in the best.

to 20 percent of total credit. This boom in consumer credit, which has led policy makers to complain that the region's financial system has been concentrating too much on financing consumption at the expense of production (de la Torre, Ize, and Schmukler 2012), is expected to continue due to a combination of increased access to banking and rapid expansion of credit cards and store cards. Three Latin American countries (Argentina, Chile, and Colombia) are ranked in the top 10 for the fastest growth in card lending debt since 2008. Store cards (retailer credit) are a relatively new phenomenon that is taking off quickly given its greater accessibility to lower-middle-class and poorer households. By one account, Brazilian families own some 181 million store cards, while Mexican families have 9 million (Capizzani, Ramírez Huerta, and Rocha e Oliveira 2012).

The combination of increased incomes and rising access to credit could significantly affect overall energy demand. Consumer durables, and hence energy

Figure 2.11 First the Fridge, Then the Washing Machine, Then the Car: The Order of Acquisition of Consumer Durables in Latin America
Percentage

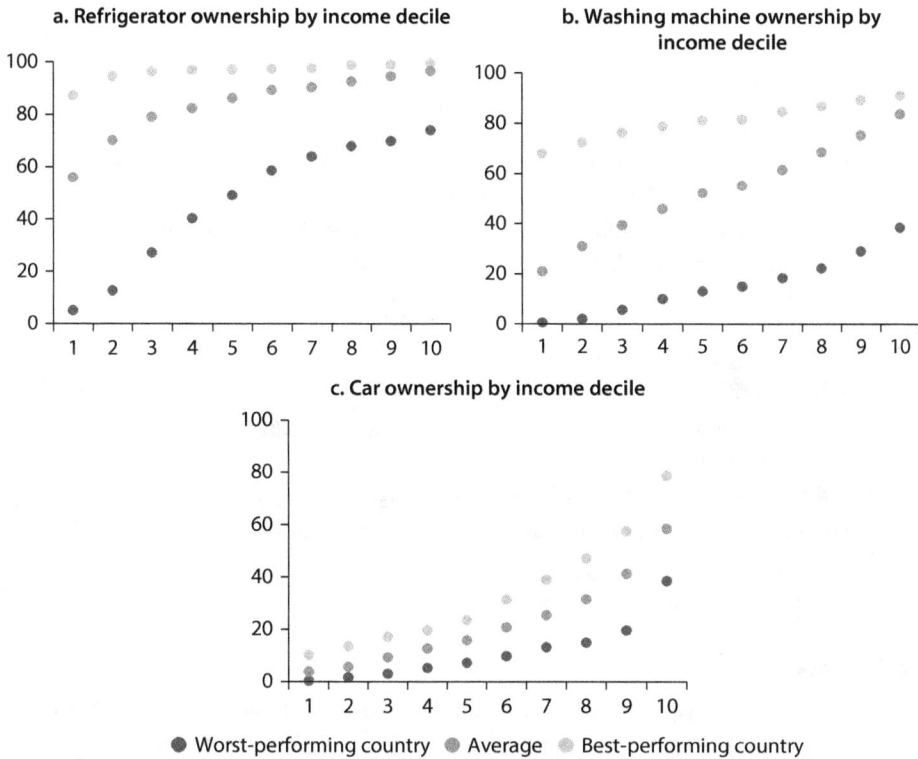

a. Refrigerator ownership by income decile

b. Washing machine ownership by income decile

c. Car ownership by income decile

● Worst-performing country ● Average ● Best-performing country

Source: Fay and Straub 2016.
Note: Deciles are defined region wide, so the figure shows how Latin Americans earning similar incomes (within a decile) may experience wide variation in access to services, depending on the country where they live. For example, the average rate of ownership of refrigerators among households in Latin America's poorest decile varies from 5 percent in the worst-performing country to 87 percent in the best.

consumption, do not increase one-to-one with income. Instead, it is generally believed that at low levels of income, increases in income have limited impact as credit-constrained households use the extra cash on basics. But as income rises, purchases of durables increase rapidly—especially if credit constraints are removed (Gertler and others 2016). Data from Latin America suggest that this is true for the poorest households, which exhibit low income elasticity for consumer durables, but that consumer behavior varies both across income groups and type of durables. Still, growth in energy demand from first-time purchases of consumer durables could have significant impacts on overall energy demand in a way that may not be sufficiently taken into account in traditional energy forecasts.

At the same time, most remaining basic access challenges in water and electricity are now concentrated in the poorest income decile. Chances are that these households are located in hard-to-reach areas—remote rural locations or difficult urban sites. They are for the most part very poor and so more likely to face affordability challenges whether for connections or for monthly service. Thus, the implication is that closing the remaining access gap could be more challenging than it has been in the past.

Notes

1. Survey conducted by the World Bank in August 2015 under the Jamaica Strategic Public Sector Transformation Project (P146688).

2. Courtesy of Diego Dorado Hernandez, based on the findings of World Bank Rapid Assessment and Action Plans conducted in Lambayeque, Peru (2013); Santa Cruz de la Sierra, Bolivia (2014); Córdoba, Argentina (2014); San Salvador, El Salvador (2014); and Colombia (2010–13).

3. This section is based on Stapledon (2012); Geurs, Boon, and Van Wee (2009); and Sandhu and others (2006).

4. The study estimated the cost to be US$3.5 billion in 2005 dollars, which is about US$4.2 billion in current (2016) dollars.

5. The urbanization part of this section is from Marulanda and others (2015) while the socioeconomic part is from Fay and Straub (2016), both background papers for this report.

References

Abiko, Alex, Luiz Reynaldo de Azevedo Cardoso, Ricardo Rinaldelli, and Heitor Cesar Riogi Haga. 2007. "Basic Costs of Slum Upgrading in Brazil." *Global Urban Development* 3 (1): 1–23.

Armendáriz, Edna, and Eduardo Contreras. 2016. "El gasto de inversión pública en América Latina: Cuánto y cuán eficiente." Presented at the Sixth Conference of the Public Investment Management Systems of Latin America and the Caribbean, San José, Costa Rica, April 19.

Balcázar, Cecilia. 2012. "Resilient Infrastructure for Sustainable Services: Latin America—Mainstreaming of Disaster Risk Management in the Water Supply and Sanitation Sector." Water and Sanitation Program, World Bank, Washington, DC.

Banerjee, Sudeshna Ghosh, Francisco Alejandro Moreno, Jonathan Edwards Sinton, Tanya Primiani, and Joonkyung Seong. 2017. *Regulatory Indicators for Sustainable Energy: A Global Scorecard for Policy Makers.* Washington, DC: World Bank. http://documents.worldbank.org/curated/en/538181487106403375/pdf/112828-REVISED-PUBLIC-RISE-2016-Report.pdf.

Briceño-Garmendia, Cecilia, Harry Moroz, and Julie Rozenberg. 2015. "Road Networks, Accessibility, and Resilience: The Cases of Colombia, Ecuador, and Peru." World Bank, Washington, DC.

Broad, Oliver, Gustavo de Moura, and Mark Howells. 2016. "Investment Needs in the Energy Sector along Multiple Socio-economic Pathways." Background paper commissioned for this report, KTH Royal Institute of Technology, Stockholm.

Cannock, Geoffrey, Jessica Silva Yon, César S. Jara Trujillo, Roberto O'Connor, and Fernando Saavedra Bonifaz. 2011. "Economic Impact of the 2007 Earthquake on the Drinking

Water and Sanitation Sector in Four Provinces of Peru: What Did Unpreparedness Cost the Country." World Bank, Washington, DC. https://www.wsp.org/sites/wsp.org/files /publications/WSP-LAC-Economic-Impact-Earthquake-Full-Study.pdf.

Capizzani, Mario, Felipe Javier Ramírez Huerta, and Paulo Rocha e Oliveira. 2012. "Consumer Credit in Latin America: Trends and Opportunities in Credit and Store Cards." Occasional Paper OP-200, IESE Business School, University of Navarra, Barcelona. http://www.iese.edu/research/pdfs/OP-0200-E.pdf.

Dabla-Norris, Era, Jim Brumby, Annette Kyobe, Zac Mills, and Chris Papageorgiou. 2012. "Investing in Public Investment: An Index of Public Investment Efficiency." IMF Working Paper 11/37, International Monetary Fund, Washington, DC. https://www .imf.org/external/pubs/ft/wp/2011/wp1137.pdf.

de la Torre, Augusto, Alain Ize, Daniel Lederman, Federico R. Bennett, and Martin Sasson. 2016. "The Big Switch in Latin America: Restoring Growth through Trade." World Bank, Washington, DC.

de la Torre, Augusto, Alain Ize, and Sergio L. Schmukler. 2012. *Financial Development in Latin America and the Caribbean: The Road Ahead*. Washington, DC: World Bank. https://openknowledge.worldbank.org/bitstream/handle/10986/2380/657440REPL ACEM0110USE0SAME0BOX0INFO.pdf?sequence=1&isAllowed=y.

Delgado, Ricardo, Angela Inés Cadena, Mónica Espinosa, Catalina Peña, and Mateo Salazar. 2014. "A Case Study on Colombian Mitigation Actions." *Climate and Development* 6: 12–24.

de Lucena, Andre Frossard Pereira, Roberto Schaeffer, and Alexandre Salem Szklo. 2010. "Least-Cost Adaptation Options for Global Climate Change Impacts on the Brazilian Electric Power System." *Global Environmental Change* 20 (2): 342–50.

de Marucci, Silvia. 2012. "The Expansion of the Panama Canal and Its Impact on Global CO_2 Emissions from Ships." *Maritime Policy and Management* 39 (6): 603–20.

Fay, Marianne, Stéphane Hallegatte, Adrien Vogt-Schilb, Julie Rozenberg, Ulf Narloch, and Tom Kerr. 2015. *Decarbonizing Development: Three Steps to a Zero-Carbon Future*. Washington, DC: World Bank. https://openknowledge.worldbank.org /handle/10986/21842.

Fay, Marianne, and Stéphane Straub. 2016. "Rising Incomes and the Demand for Infrastructure of Latin American Households." Background paper commissioned for this report, World Bank, Washington, DC.

Ferreira, Francisco H. G., Julian Messina, Jamele Rigolini, Luis-Felipe López-Calva, Maria Ana Lugo, and Renos Vakis. 2012. *Economic Mobility and the Rise of the Latin American Middle Class*. Washington, DC: World Bank. https://openknowledge.worldbank.org /handle/10986/11858.

Gertler, Paul J., Orie Shelef, Catherine D. Wolfram, and Alan Fuchs. 2016. "The Demand for Energy-Using Assets among the World's Rising Middle Classes." *American Economic Review* 106 (6): 1366–401.

Geurs, Karst T., Wouter Boon, and Bert Van Wee. 2009. "Social Impacts of Transport: Literature Review and the State of the Practice of Transport Appraisal in the Netherlands and the United Kingdom." *Transport Reviews* 29 (1): 69–90.

Hunja, Robert. 2012. "E-Procurement: Opportunities and Challenges." Presented at Electronic Procurement: Challenges and Opportunities, European Commission, Brussels, June 26. http://ec.europa.eu/geninfo/query/resultaction.jsp?swlang=en&Qu eryText=robert+hunja+procurement&sbtSearch=Search.

Inostroza, Luis, Rolf Baur, and Elmar Csaplovics. 2010. "Urban Sprawl and Fragmentation in Latin America: A Comparison with European Cities—The Myth of the Diffuse Latin American City." Working paper, Lincoln Institute of Land Policy, Cambridge, MA. http://docplayer.net/2719326-Urban-sprawl-and-fragmentation-in-latin-america-a-comparison-with-european-cities-the-myth-of-the-diffuse-latin-american-city.html.

IPCC (Intergovernmental Panel on Climate Change). 2014. *Climate Change 2014: Impacts, Adaptation, and Vulnerability—Part A: Global and Sectoral Aspects*. New York: Cambridge University Press.

Kalra, Nidhi, David G. Groves, Laura Bonzanigo, Cayo Ramos, Brandon Enrique Carter, Iván Rodriguez Cabanillas, and Edmundo Molina Perez. 2015. "Robust Decision-Making in the Water Sector: A Strategy for Implementing Lima's Long-Term Water Resources Master Plan." Policy Research Working Paper 7439, World Bank, Washington, DC.

Kalra, Nidhi, Stéphane Hallegatte, Robert J. Lempert, Casey Brown, Adrian Fozzard, Stuart Gill, and Ankur Shah. 2014. "Agreeing on Robust Decisions: New Processes for Decision-Making under Deep Uncertainty." Policy Research Working Paper 6906, World Bank, Washington, DC. http://documents.worldbank.org/curated/en/3650314 68338971343/pdf/WPS6906.pdf.

Kim, Yoonhee, and Bontje Zangerling, eds. 2016. *Mexico Urbanization Review: Managing Spatial Growth for Productive and Livable Cities in Mexico*. Washington, DC: World Bank.

Lempert, Robert J., Steven W. Popper, David G. Groves, Nidhi Kalra, Jordan R. Fischbach, Steven C. Bankes, and Benjamin P. Bryant. 2013. "Making Good Decisions without Predictions: Robust Decision Making for Planning under Deep Uncertainty." Research Brief 9701, RAND, Washington, DC. http://www.rand.org/pubs/research_briefs /RB9701.html.

Libertun de Duren, Nora, and Roberto Guerrero Compéan. 2016. "Growing Resources for Growing Cities: Density and the Cost of Municipal Public Services in Latin America." *Urban Studies* 53 (14): 3082–107.

Litman, Todd. 2015. "Analysis of Public Policies That Unintentionally Encourage and Subsidize Urban Sprawl." Victoria Transport Policy Institute, London. http://static .newclimateeconomy.report/wp-content/uploads/2015/03/public-policies -encourage-sprawl-nce-report.pdf.

Magrin, Graciela O., José A. Marengo, Jean-Phillipe Boulanger, Marcos S. Buckeridge, Edwin Castellanos, Germán Poveda, Fabio R. Scarano, and Sebastián Vicuña. 2014. "Central and South America." In *Climate Change 2014: Impacts, Adaptation, and Vulnerability—Part B: Regional Aspects*, edited by Vicente R. Barros, Christopher B. Field, David Jon Dokken, Michael D. Mastrandrea, Katharine J. Mach, T. Eren Bilir, Monalisa Chatterjee, Kristie L. Ebi, Yuka Otsuki Estrada, Robert C. Genova, Betelhem Girma, Andrew N. Levy, Sandy MacCracken, Patricia R. Mastrandrea, and Leslie L. White, 1499–566. New York: Cambridge University Press.

Marulanda, Catalina, Beatriz Eraso, Emanuela Monteiro, and Pablo Gluzmann. 2015. "LAC Infrastructure Gap: A Territorial Development Perspective." Background paper commissioned for this report, World Bank, Washington, DC.

Miralles-Wilhelm, Fernando. 2016. "Water Security and Infrastructure for Development in Latin American and the Caribbean 2050." Background paper commissioned for this report, World Bank, Washington, DC.

Peña, L. C., A. Miranda Velázquez, and M. Gómez Torrez. 2015. *IDEAL 2014. La infrae-structura en el desarrollo de América Latina. Infraestructura y cambio climático.* Bogotá: CAF. http://scioteca.caf.com/handle/123456789/748.

Perrotti, Daniel E., and Mariana Vera Rueda. 2015. "Avances y retos de los Sistemas Nacionales de Inversión Publica de América Latina: Resultados de la encuesta 2014." Gestión Pública 83, Comisión Económica para América Latina y el Caribe, United Nations, Santiago. http://repositorio.cepal.org/bitstream/handle/11362/37862/1/S1500113_es.pdf

Reguero, Borja G., Iñigo J. Losada, Pedro Díaz-Simal, Fernando J. Méndez, and Michael W. Beck. 2015. "Effects of Climate Change on Exposure to Coastal Flooding in Latin America and the Caribbean." *PLoS One* 10 (7): e0133409. http://journals.plos.org/plosone/article?id=10.1371/journal.pone.0133409.

Sandhu, Sonia Chand, Mridula Singh, Tapas Paul, S. Vaideeswaran, and R. Viswanathan. 2006. *Management of Environment and Social Issues in Highway Projects in India.* Washington, DC: World Bank. http://documents.worldbank.org/curated/en/313631468042034171/pdf/39752.pdf.

Serebrisky, Tomás, Ancor Suárez-Alemán, Diego Margot, and Maria Cecilia Ramirez. 2015. "Financing Infrastructure in Latin America and the Caribbean: How, How Much, and by Whom?" Inter-American Development Bank, Washington, DC. https://publications.iadb.org/bitstream/handle/11319/7315/Infrastructure%20Financing.%20Definitivo.pdf?sequence=1.

Stapledon, Tony. 2012. *Why Infrastructure Sustainability Is Good for Your Business.* Brisbane, Australia: Cooperative Research Centre for Infrastructure and Engineering Asset Management.

UN-Habitat (United Nations Human Settlements Programme). 2013. *Planning and Design for Sustainable Urban Mobility: Global Report on Human Settlements 2013.* New York: Routledge. http://unhabitat.org/?mbt_book=planning-and-design-for-sustainable-urban-mobility-global-report-on-human-settlements-2013.

Vergara, Walter, Ana R. Rios, Luis M. Galindo, Pablo Gutman, Paul Isbell, Paul H. Suding, and Joseluis Samaniego. 2013. *The Climate and Development Challenge for Latin America and the Caribbean: Options for Climate-Resilient, Low-Carbon Development.* Washington, DC: Inter-American Development Bank.

Vogt-Schilb, Adrien, Stéphane Hallegatte, and Christophe de Gouvello. 2015. "Marginal Abatement Cost Curves and the Quality of Emission Reductions: A Case Study on Brazil." *Climate Policy* 15 (6): 703–23.

Ward, Philip J., Kenneth M. Strzepek, W. Pieter Pauw, Luke M. Brander, Gordon A. Hughes, and Jeroen C. J. H Aerts. 2010. "Partial Costs of Global Climate Change Adaptation for the Supply of Raw Industrial and Municipal Water: A Methodology and Application." *Environmental Research Letters* 5 (4): 44011.

World Bank. 2008. *Costa Rica: Public Expenditure Review—Enhancing the Efficiency of Expenditures.* Washington, DC: World Bank. https://hubs.worldbank.org/docs/imagebank/pages/docprofile.aspx?nodeid=9543594

———. 2010. "The Costs to Developing Countries of Adapting to Climate Change: New Methods and Estimates." World Bank, Washington, DC.

———. 2012a. "International Bank for Reconstruction and Development Program Document for a Proposed Loan in the Amount of US$300 Million to the State of Rio de Janeiro with a Guarantee of the Federative Republic of Brazil for a Fiscal

Efficiency for Quality of Public Service Delivery Development Policy Loan." World Bank, Washington, DC. http://documents.worldbank.org/curated/en/979281468 229179151/pdf/627930REVISED00Official0Use0Only090.pdf.

———. 2012b. *Public Expenditure Review for Peru: Spending for Results*. Washington, DC: World Bank. http://documents.worldbank.org/curated/en/225811468297875669 /pdf/NonAsciiFileName0.pdf.

———. 2013a. "Honduras: Managing Fiscal and Public Finance Challenges." World Bank, Washington, DC.

———. 2013b. "Inclusive Green Growth in Latin America and the Caribbean." World Bank, Washington, DC.

———. 2013c. "Mexico Moves to Results-based Procurement System." World Bank, Washington, DC. http://beta.worldbank.org/en/results/2013/04/03/mexico-moves -to-results-based-procurement-system.

———. 2013d. *Towards Better Expenditure Quality: Guatemala Public Expenditure Review*. Washington, DC: World Bank. https://openknowledge.worldbank.org/handle /10986/16085.

———. 2014a. "Ceara PforR: Full Fiduciary Systems Assessment." World Bank, Washington, DC. http://documents.worldbank.org/curated/en/346981468238750993/pdf/89279 0WP0P12080ry0Assessment0final.pdf.

———. 2014b. "Program Appraisal Document on a Proposed Loan in the Amount US$55 Million to the National Bank of Public Works and Services (BANOBRAS) with the Guarantee of the United Mexican States for Oaxaca Water and Sanitation Sector Modernization Operation Project." World Bank, Washington, DC. http://documents. worldbank.org/curated/en/451781468123256085/pdf/871040PAD0P145010Box38 5211B00OUO090.pdf.

———. 2014c. *Turn Down the Heat: Confronting the New Climate Normal*. Washington, DC: World Bank.

———. 2016. "Better Spending, Better Services: A Review of Public Finances in Haiti—Overview." World Bank, Washington, DC. https://openknowledge.worldbank .org/handle/10986/24690.

———. Forthcoming a. *Energy Markets in LAC: Emerging Disruptions and the Next Frontier*. Washington, DC: World Bank.

———. Forthcoming b. Strengthening Governance in Infrastructure in Brazil. Washington, DC: World Bank.

———. 2017. *Benchmarking Public Procurement 2017*. World Bank, Washington, DC. http://bpp.financeandprivatesector.org/~/media/WBG/BPP/Documents/Reports/Ben chmarking-Public-Procurement-2017.pdf.

WRI (World Resources Institute). 2016. "CAIT Country Greenhouse Gas Emissions: Sources and Methods." WRI, Washington, DC.

CHAPTER 3

The Road Ahead: Spending Better to Meet "Real" Infrastructure Needs

Chapter 1 started by discussing Latin America's infrastructure investment needs. Needs are usually defined based on the historical relationship between income and infrastructure growth. So let us look at the region's road ahead if countries maintain the historical link between infrastructure access and income growth, assuming a high-growth scenario similar to the 2002–12 one—but go a step further, using decile-specific access rates to see how different income groups are likely to fare given that, in most countries, public policies favor richer households.

The results are sobering. If the road ahead is anything like the one behind, it will take the region between 10 and 50 years to achieve universal coverage in electricity, up to 90 years for water, and a staggering 200 years for sanitation (Fay and Straub 2016). The value of the elasticity of access with respect to income plays a crucial role here. Consider the three countries with about 50 percent coverage rates for water at the bottom of the income distribution—Bolivia, the Dominican Republic, and Peru. The fact that Peru is much better than Bolivia in translating income growth into improved access (as shown by their respective elasticities of 0.18 and 0.08) means that Peru is likely to achieve full coverage for the poorest decile in half the time (43 years as opposed to 96; admittedly still a very long time).

But these are constrained elasticities, capturing a combination of constrained demand (largely due to lack of income) and constrained supply (due to limited or inefficient public investments). It is probably more useful to think of the potential margin of adjustment to tackle the last-mile challenge as being the improvement in the elasticity that could be achieved through additional or more efficient investment. For example, improving spending to increase the income elasticity to 0.2 (that is, above the current regional best performer) would allow the nine best-performing countries to connect all the households in the first decile to water in less than 21 years. An even higher elasticity of 0.5 would allow all countries except El Salvador to complete that task in 16 years or less.

So what to do? Are we back to the starting point of the report, with estimates of investment needs that argue for Latin America to spend a lot more than it does? More money would make things easier. But is that an option?

The discussion of fiscal space in chapter 2 makes it abundantly clear that governments in the region have limited room to increase public investments. Over the past 16 years, total public investment has been 3.1–4.6 percent of gross domestic product (GDP). Today it is about 3.4 percent. On average, only about a third of this public investment goes to infrastructure. So, going forward, it is unlikely that public investment in infrastructure will be much above 1.0–1.5 percent of GDP.

As for public-private partnerships (PPPs), the discussion in chapter 1 showed that while PPPs account for about 40 percent of Latin America's infrastructure investments, they depend heavily on government support: about one-third of their financing comes from public sources, and about one-half of all deals receive some type of government guarantee. In other words, constrained public finance also means constrained private finance for infrastructure. Although the region has had a few extraordinary years, private participation in infrastructure has usually hovered between 0.5 and 1.0 percent of GDP.

So at the most, the region is unlikely to see investments in infrastructure from traditional sources exceed 1.5–2.5 percent of GDP in the near future. This means that the main way forward, at least in the short to medium term, is to make scarce resources stretch further and improve the access of public service providers to commercial finance. That can be done by reducing the tab associated with investment spending "needs" by focusing on priorities, managing demand, reducing costs, and improving public spending (and public enterprise) efficiency more generally. Fortunately, as noted throughout this report, Latin America has plenty of scope to do this.

Focusing on Priorities—Setting the Right Goals Is Essential

There is no such thing as an absolute investment need. The amount of money needed for Latin American infrastructure depends on the goals that are set and on how efficient investors are at achieving them. So, a sensible approach to defining infrastructure investment needs must start by defining goals—in terms of the access, quality, affordability, sustainability, and inclusiveness of infrastructure services that are needed to achieve the region's development ambition.

As such, the received wisdom that Latin America "needs" to spend 4–5 percent of GDP on infrastructure is not helpful. In fact, it is outright distracting. Instead, countries should conduct their own analyses to define their goals and what it would take to achieve them. Unfortunately, few countries in the region have developed clear goals—and even fewer have priced them or examined whether they have the resources or institutions to develop strategic plans, as opposed to wish lists.

Yet doing so would be highly instructive. Take water and sanitation. A careful analysis of water and investment needs done at the World Bank (Hutton and Varughese 2016) started by defining two possible goals. One was the Millennium

Development Goal (MDG) of achieving universal access to basic water, sanitation, and hygiene by 2030; the other was the much more ambitious Sustainable Development Goal (SDG) of achieving universal access to *safely managed* water and sanitation services by 2030.

The difference in ambition between these two goals has striking implications for their cost. Providing basic access to everyone in the region would cost a mere 0.05 percent of GDP a year through 2030; achieving universal access to *safely managed* water and sanitation would cost five times more, or about 0.25 percent of GDP. (This 0.25 percent happens to be what Latin America currently spends on water and sanitation. As such, the region should be able to achieve ambitious goals without necessarily increasing capital spending.)

How the region goes about pursuing this goal will make a big difference. There is lots of uncertainty in these kinds of estimates—about population, level of urbanization, and costs. And there are choices, some to do with the analysis (what discount rate to use?) and some to do with the strategy, notably the path chosen to get there. The 0.25 percent of GDP assumes that about half of households will go straight to a higher level of service and half will first pass through basic water and unimproved sanitation. If all first go through the low-cost technology and later upgrade, overall costs would be higher. Thus, analysis provides low and high estimates: a low discount rate and a population that immediately obtains the higher level of services results in an estimated 0.1 percent of GDP a year "investment need," while the higher discount rate and indirect path to the SDG would raise the estimated cost to some 0.4 percent of GDP.

Similarly, and as discussed in the section on climate change, investment "needs" for electricity depend on the goals set and the strategy adopted to achieve them. According to modeling done for this study, a business-as-usual investment path that follows South America countries' master plans, with demand growing as in recent years and an unchanged climate, would entail annual investments of US$23 billion to US$24 billion a year (Broad, de Moura, and Howells 2016). A scenario with much greater penetration of renewables would be somewhat more expensive at US$25 billion to US$26 billion per year. But an ambitious "disruptive scenario" that adopts smart grids, smart metering (and hence effective demand-side management), and ambitious penetration of renewables would cost US$8 billion to US$9 billion a year. This does not include the cost of demand-side management programs, so the final tab would be higher—but the point remains that how the region goes about implementing its energy strategy will have a significant impact on how much is needed.

Interestingly, these numbers are well within the range of what the region has been spending on energy (0.75–1.00 percent of GDP), even when adding the cost of expanding access to electricity and modern cooking fuels: expressed as a percentage of South America's current GDP, the disruptive scenario would amount to 0.2 percent of GDP (not counting demand-side management investments) and the business-as-usual scenario, 0.6 percent. In other words, an ambitious, clean, and equitable energy goal, well conceived and delivered, is achievable within the current spending envelope.

Rethinking Infrastructure in Latin America and the Caribbean
http://dx.doi.org/10.1596/978-1-4648-1101-2

That leaves transport, which is far more complicated. First, what goals should be set? There must be at least three: one for urban transport, one for rural transport, and one for freight. But how to set them? Unlike for water, sanitation, electricity, or modern cooking fuels, there can be no presumption that universal access should be the goal for any of these. Nor is it even clear what universal access would mean for urban, rural, or freight transport. Further, there is no good database on any of these three dimensions to allow us to estimate how far the region is from whatever goals are set.

As such, every country will need to define its transport goals and develop a master plan. The few master plans that exist tend to be wish lists and overly focused on infrastructure as opposed to services. Good roads, well-maintained rail tracks, modern airports, and dredged waterways are important, but competitive, well-priced, and well-regulated trucking, bus, rail, and aviation companies and good multimodal integration are at least as critical. Good transport infrastructure is expensive—so a focus on the service side and on spending efficiency is essential. And as the section on spending efficiency showed, transport has massive potential for increased efficiency.

Infrastructure goals are best defined in terms of the service needed—say, mobility—rather than the input required—say, kilometers of roads. This approach opens up the possibility of managing demand to reduce the cost of satisfying this demand. Thus, as discussed earlier, denser cities enhance mobility at much lower cost. Rough estimates are that encouraging compact development instead of sprawl can reduce overall infrastructure construction and service costs by 10–40 percent (Marulanda and others 2015).

Much can be achieved through demand-side management. The discussion on investment "needs" in energy shows that demand-side management largely determines how much investment will really be needed—and "negawatts" (energy saved from energy efficiency and demand-side management efforts) are almost always cheaper than megawatts. And here pricing services adequately has a double-whammy effect: it encourages efficient use by consumers (to buy more fuel-efficient cars, use public transportation, turn off lights, buy energy-efficient appliances, fix leaking faucets, and so on), and generates resources, thereby reducing the burden on taxpayers and scarce public funds.

Improving Utility Performance and Deploying Public and Concessional Finance Where It Is Truly Needed

Pricing services appropriately and running utilities efficiently also makes it possible for them to attract private financing. In 2016, only 20 percent of the Latin American water utilities included in the International Benchmarking Network for Water and Sanitation Utilities (IBNET) database covered their operations and maintenance costs and generated enough of a surplus to mobilize commercial borrowing (assumed to be cash revenues exceeding costs by at least 20 percent). This means that 80 percent of utilities would have difficulties mobilizing commercial financing unless they implement significant reforms to improve cost recovery.

But if few can attract commercial financing now, the potential for improvement is significant. Using this same dataset, the average level of reported non-revenue water (water that is delivered into a network but "lost" before it reaches a legitimate consumer) was 31 percent. But there were significant variations in performance: the top 10 percent of performers achieved nonrevenue water levels of 15 percent, while the level among the lowest decile was 57 percent. In terms of collection efficiency, the average for the dataset was 75 percent of the amount billed, whereas the average in the top decile was 100 percent and in the lowest decile, 46 percent. Assuming that utilities could achieve the performance of utilities in the top decile in terms of collection efficiency (Step 1 in figure 3.1), that modest nonlabor efficiency gains (predominantly energy) of 15 percent can be made (Step 2), that leakage levels could be reduced to 25 percent (realistic and less than the top decile), and that water saved from leaks can be sold at the prevailing average tariff (Step 3), then 65 percent of the region's utilities in the IBNET sample could create sufficient surplus to mobilize commercial borrowing.[1]

The implication is that reasonable progress in efficient management could more than triple the number of water utilities with potential access to commercial financing. In this simplified model (up to Step 3), the financial improvements are achieved at current tariff levels. If the utility can enhance its revenue stream from tariffs, taxes, or a mix of the two (Step 4), then 82 percent of

Figure 3.1 With Reasonable Progress on Better Management, Four Times as Many Utilities Could Access Commercial Financing

Percentage of utilities considered creditworthy

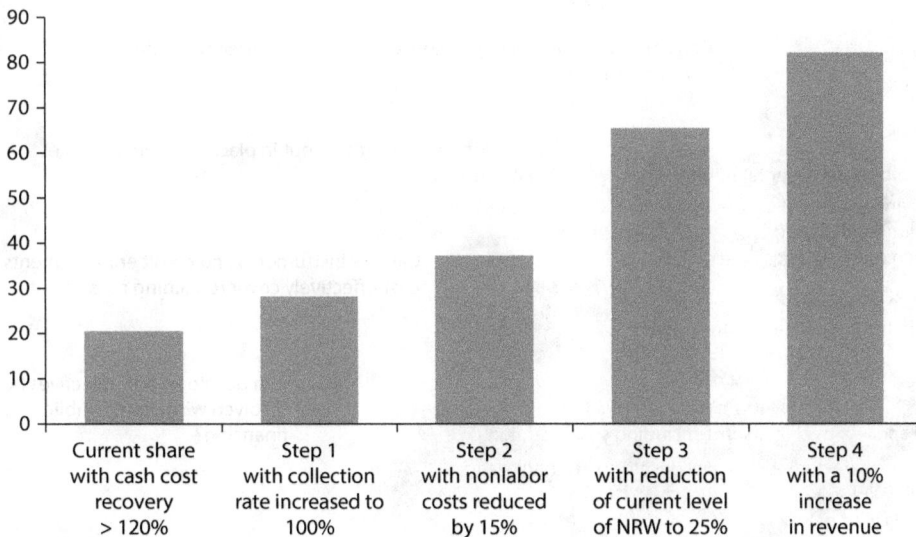

Source: Courtesy of William Kingdom and Alexander Danilenko (World Bank) based on IBNET database 2016.
Note: NRW = nonrevenue water, or water that is produced but "lost" before it reaches the consumer.

Rethinking Infrastructure in Latin America and the Caribbean
http://dx.doi.org/10.1596/978-1-4648-1101-2

utilities would achieve the 120 percent cost recovery level. Mobilizing funds up front to deliver such efficiency gains would be needed, as would capacity building. But if these cash surpluses could be maintained or increased over the long term through good policies, governance, and incentives, the ability to mobilize commercial financing starts to look like a distinct possibility. This could well lead to a virtuous circle: the lure of external financing—and the scrutiny of external investors—would motivate utilities to be efficient, and the additional financing would then enable them to invest and provide a service good enough that consumers would be willing to pay for it.

Commercial Financing and the Importance of Making Judicious Use of Public Resources

Increased reliance on commercial financing, where possible and appropriate, along with the judicious use of public and concessional resources, is one of the essential ways through which Latin American countries can "spend better." To do so, the World Bank is recommending a simple sequential decision-making framework (figure 3.2).

The starting point of this approach is that any investment project or program that *can* be financed on commercial terms while remaining affordable and offering value for money, *should be.*[2] Where commercial financing is not cost effective or viable because of perceived risks or market failures, efforts should focus on addressing these market failures through upstream reforms to strengthen country and sector policies, regulations, and institutions or targeted public interventions (for example, targeted subsidies or complementary public

Figure 3.2 A Decision-Making Framework to Ensure the Judicious Use of Scarce Public and Concessional Finance

Source: World Bank 2017.
Note: DFI = development finance institutions; MDB = multilateral development bank; SWF = sovereign wealth fund.

investments such as transmission lines). Where risks remain high and raise the cost of commercial capital beyond that afforded by project or corporate revenue generation, it may still be possible to cost-effectively use risk-sharing instruments backed by public or concessional finance to lower the cost of commercial capital. If commercial financing is still not viable or cost effective, then public and concessional resources are the likely solution.

Importantly, this framework can only be applied to services that can be charged to users, as user fees are what creates the basis for commercial financing options beyond the use of general taxes.[3] A very rough estimate by the World Bank estimates that perhaps up to 50 percent of infrastructure investment needs could theoretically be financed on a commercial basis, based on the feasibility and desirability of different subsectors to generate user fees. Feasibility depends on the ability to tie a service to an individual user (easier for electricity than for rural roads), whereas desirability will vary depending on externalities, the need for demand-side management, and social or political economy considerations. And of course, willingness to pay will also matter for cost recovery—users are more likely to accept charges for good quality services and rates perceived to be fair.

Equity and poverty concerns are not at odds with reliance on commercial financing, even as they are often invoked in arguments against full cost recovery for basic services such as water and sanitation, electricity, public transport, and modern cooking fuels. The needs of the poor are in fact typically best served by a combination of cost-recovery tariffs and targeted subsidies and payments schemes adapted to the needs of the poor. Most of the wealthier Latin American countries have well-developed social registries and safety nets (for example, Brazil, Chile, Colombia, Mexico) but the targeting is likely to be a challenge for countries without such systems. Still, efforts at targeting the poor are likely to help them more than underfunded, low-cost recovery utilities unable to expand coverage or provide quality service.

Nevertheless, it may be difficult to reconcile the higher return expectations of commercial financing requirements with affordability concerns. This is particularly true in island states where the cost of infrastructure service provision such as power generation may already be high for reasons of economic geography. It is also an issue for countries and sectors with low access rates where the consumer base is too small to bear the cost of service expansion (hence prohibiting full cost pricing). Fortunately, this is only a challenge in a few countries in the region (for example, Haiti) and sectors with low coverage (wastewater treatment and modern cooking fuels). In such cases, the solution typically involves a blend of financing tools—commercial, public, and concessionary—to match the conditions that the investments face.

Applying this framework to judiciously deploy scarce public and concessional resources and ensuring commercial financing provides value for money is not always simple. It implies carefully weighing the trade-offs between the financing of infrastructure on the back of government taxes versus commercial financing backed by the securitization of user fees. While public and concessional financing appears cheaper than commercial sources of finance, it is drawn from a pool of scarce resources whose opportunity cost should be carefully considered with each investment decision. As for commercial capital (which includes the cost of any guarantee, off-take agreements, and any government-backed credit agreement), its higher cost must be weighed against potential efficiency gains in the provision of the asset.

Corporatization and the Importance of Improving the Performance of Utilities—Public and Private

So how to obtain such efficiency improvements? Some countries and sectors have turned to the private sector for service delivery, with the result that the number of connections served via private participation in infrastructure (PPI) increased from 11 percent in 1995 to around 60 percent by 2006 for electricity (but are still only 8 percent for water).[4] A review of more than 250 electricity distribution companies and more than 1,700 water and sanitation utilities in Latin America found that on average, private utilities outperform public ones, although there are good and bad performers in both groups (the top 10 percent of public utilities outperform the average private utility) (Andrés, Schwartz, and Guasch 2013). The conclusion of the review was that, *when carefully designed and implemented*, private participation in service provision improves sector performance—specifically labor productivity, efficiency, and service quality.

The caveat about careful design and implementation is important. As Andrés, Schwartz, and Guasch (2013) point out, improving sector performance demands that key determinants such as ownership structure, regulatory governance, and corporate governance be addressed strategically, not in isolation. Private management or ownership of a utility is no silver bullet—private participation is unlikely to yield the desired efficiency gains in the absence of some type of market test—and Latin America is rife with examples of costly and failed PPPs. Similar experiences have led Organisation for Economic Co-operation and Development (OECD) countries to adopt a number of principles aiming to ensure affordability, value for money, and transparency.[5]

A companion report on PPPs in Latin America (Garcia-Kilroy and Rudolph 2017) finds that the region has significant potential to increase PPPs but insists on the fact that PPPs are not a silver bullet. Even in advanced economies with successful programs, PPPs seldom exceed 10–15 percent of total infrastructure finance. PPPs should not be used as an off-balance sheet financing instrument to bypass fiscal constraints. Instead, the rationale for PPPs should be to achieve value for money for the government. Finally, effective PPPs require sophisticated institutions to implement them as well as a minimum level of financial sector development.

The report argues that achieving Latin America's potential in terms of PPPs will require tackling the following challenges:

- *Often weak underpinnings.* This includes: (1) *PPP frameworks*, where they exist, are still facing important challenges on issues such as quality project selection and structuring, risk allocation between the public and the private sector, and procurement procedures; (2) *project finance skills*, which are at the core of PPP financing, are underdeveloped among banks, and financial regulations seldom acknowledge the difference with corporate lending; (3) *depth and sophistication of local financial markets (banks or capital markets)*, whose size and sophistication are insufficient to address financing gaps or facilitate adequate risk sharing between government and other stakeholders.

- *Low participation of foreign sponsors and financiers* who can provide volume, competition, and knowledge transfer.
- *A lack of consensus* among public and private sector stakeholders around PPP frameworks and programs, which is critical to reach the necessary trust among the different parties.

The report offers a useful reminder that PPP programs are not right for all countries. Only large and medium-size countries with a minimum threshold of financial development would be able to afford PPP programs in local currency. For smaller countries, PPPs could be a relevant source of financing for select signature projects with revenues in dollars, but most would need concessional financing or guarantees from multilateral development finance institutions (DFIs) to access international capital. The experience of the region has been of a small presence of multilateral DFIs. As to domestic DFIs that have been active financiers of infrastructure, they have tended to prioritize direct lending instead of assuming a catalytic role to mobilize private financing.

But whether utilities and service providers are public, private, or a mix, they need to be run as corporatized entities and regulated by independent regulatory agencies that are transparent, accountable, and free of political interference. Key findings and conclusions of the review of Latin America's electricity distribution companies and water and sanitation utilities (Andrés, Schwartz, and Guasch 2013) include the following:

- The presence of a regulatory agency significantly improves sector performance, raises labor productivity and cost recovery, and reduces operational expenses and distribution losses.
- Improving sector performance demands that key determinants—such as ownership structure, regulatory governance, and corporate governance—be addressed strategically, not in isolation. Private management or ownership of a utility is no silver bullet.
- For state-owned enterprises (SOEs), strong accountability is central to improving performance. Corporate governance standards (which are the norm for privatized or privately managed utilities), performance orientation, and professional management were found to be the most important determinants of performance. More generally, best practices for any utility or corporatized service provider include an independent, performance-driven board; a corporate structure that prevents political interference; a professional staff; clear disclosure policies; and mechanisms to evaluate and reward performance.

- Reform success requires addressing the technical and financial dimensions of the reform (concession laws and contracts that clearly assign and mitigate risks, discourage opportunistic bidding and renegotiations, and are embedded in transparent and predictable regulatory systems that promote efficiency and accountability and address social concerns).
- Reform success also necessitates addressing legitimate social concerns and perceptions. Reversal of policies can be triggered by popular discontent associated with a failure to help those most affected (for example, through targeted subsidies to protect the poor against necessary tariff hikes or job search assistance for redundant employees of a utility) but also by a failure to communicate success.

There are many examples of utilities and other service providers that have turned around and become good performers—but this often requires a combination of a catalytic event that creates a space for reform and savvy political and technical leaders that seize the opportunity to formulate a mutually beneficial partnership. Together they must help shape networks and alliances for change and start to embed the reform legacy. But success is only possible if the balance of political economy pay-offs remains in favor of reform, and, once achieved, in favor of sustained good service, even as the attractions of predation on the utility increase. Experience points to steps reformers can take to ensure lasting success (box 3.1). And while these findings were derived in the context of an analysis of utilities, they apply equally well to any infrastructure service provider.

Box 3.1 The Political Economy of Reform: Conditions for Change

A review of successful water sector reforms found that building reform momentum and sustaining service required action on three interrelated fronts, including the following:

- **Building and strengthening internal capacity and culture:** The technocratic and managerial skills that helped launch the reforms were then used to build strong staff and managers. Other managerial techniques—like performance-based pay, inclusive corporate strategic planning, and general transparency—also helped build and strengthen performance-based cultures. Utility leaders built internal capabilities and cultures that made the utility successful and later on helped to sustain reforms. A professional culture provided a barrier against predation on the utility since, being anathema to professional culture, the organization itself would fight against it. Grooming future leaders and promoting training and development were particularly important in the cases studied. This is an indication that leadership is a critical variable, not solely at the outset of reforms, but throughout the life of a successful utility, particularly in a precarious macropolitical economy context. By creating a deep management bench, a utility reduces the risk that losing a leader will undo its success. A performance-based corporate culture, with an emphasis on transparency, also promoted reform momentum and reform resilience.

box continues next page

Box 3.1 The Political Economy of Reform: Conditions for Change *(continued)*

A performance-based pay system—based on annual reviews against performance indicators derived from the utility's overall mission, and well-defined job descriptions for staff—is important in many of the case utilities. Many utilities also involve all staff in strategic planning. This sets the scene for establishing ownership of the institution, with staff at all levels able to understand, able to operationalize, and able to articulate the approach taken by the management.

- **Forging and embedding alliances with external stakeholders:** Alliances with customers, the government, development partners, and other stakeholders were used to build momentum for reform and help sustain it. Utility leaders demonstrated a high degree of political savvy, understanding of the political and wider sociocultural context, and the ability to navigate competing interests in an unsettled governance and institutional environment. Alliances constructed in the momentum phase were instrumental in maintaining reforms later.
- **Creating and strengthening formal rules and structures (institutions):** In isolation, formal rules and structures are an inadequate guarantee of sustained success. "Independent" boards, for example, are routinely replaced by politicians, sometimes in breach of company law. "Independent" regulators may be reluctant to approve tariff increases. But when coupled with professionally capable organizations embedded in a web of stakeholder alliances, formal regulatory and governance structures can contribute to the sustainability of reforms.

Source: Heymans and others 2016.

___

Improving Public Investment Management and Spending Efficiency

According to the International Monetary Fund (IMF), reducing inefficiencies in developing countries' public investment (including but not limited to infrastructure) by 2030 would provide the same boost to capital stock as increasing government investment by 5 percentage points of GDP in emerging economies and by 14 percentage points of GDP in low-income countries (IMF 2014). These types of estimates are fairly heroic, but they do suggest that public investment efficiency gains can have more than microlevel effects. In addition, more efficient countries are likely to be more attractive to investors interested in PPPs. In fact, evidence suggests that PPI flows are sensitive to the investment climate—more so than direct foreign investment in general (Araya, Schwartz, and Andrés 2013).

There are many ways to improve public investment efficiency. In order of importance, these include the following:

Build effective public sector institutions with clear mandates. A critical factor in a country's ability to spend efficiently on well-identified priorities is the strength of its institutions (Andrés, Biller, and Dappe 2016). Where decision makers ignore the results of prioritization exercises, or where regulatory institutions cannot weigh in with checks and balances to block questionable projects, even the best methodologies will be of little use. So a priority for infrastructure in the region is to strengthen the institutions and systems relevant to transport, electricity, and water and sanitation investments as follows:

- Central government institutions, such as a ministry of finance or planning, need to take responsibility for facilitating an overall infrastructure strategy that is based on sound analysis, prioritization, and political mandate.
- Sector institutions must have the capacity to identify, prioritize, and implement projects according to politically endorsed sector priorities and visions.
- Major administrative systems such as planning procedures, budgeting rules, treasury operations, procurement procedures, human resources, and safeguard systems must be aligned with the needs of capital investment projects (rather than being narrowly focused on controlling cash expenditures) to ensure efficiency, effectiveness, and transparency around investment.

Such public sector capacities are critical to enable the development of an overall national investment plan, a politically sanctioned short list of projects, and an overall policy on how to use private sector expertise and innovation in the development of the national infrastructure framework. Infrastructure Australia offers an interesting example of such an approach (box 3.2).

- *Include multiyear budgeting in project selection and budgeting.* This ensures resources are available for operations and maintenance, donor-funded projects are included in the budget, and that the public has access to key fiscal information.
- *Allow for project scrutiny by the legislature and public.* Greater transparency regarding the key feasibility, cost/benefit analysis, and tendering and contract documents, as well as the use of independent evaluators, can hamper pork barrel politics. Audit and evaluation should include ex-post evaluation and external audits, as well as, importantly, the existence of an asset register or inventory of public property. Findings should be made public.
- *Ensure budgetary rules work to strengthen good project execution, rather than just control spending.* Government agencies should be allowed to carry over project funds from year to year. This would help reduce pressures to inappropriately expedite procurement and address the fact that the dry season, which is the optimal time for most public works, typically spans two fiscal years. Budgeting funds to investment programs in large blocks also strengthens good capital management as it allows agencies to switch funds from projects that are going slowly to those that are ahead of schedule or are more pressing. Portfolio budgeting also prevents the private contractors from knowing what the government expects to pay for a contract, thereby turning it into a bid floor.
- *Use objective criteria and analysis to help decision makers prioritize among the multiplicity of projects across all sectors.* Unfortunately, Latin American governments seldom have the resources and data to do a full-fledged analysis, but

multicriteria analysis can be used with some basic project appraisal data to rank a multitude of projects (see Marcelo and others 2016; and Andrés, Biller, and Dappe 2016 for methodologies). This is likely to work best where decision criteria, weighting, and sensitivity analysis are decided in advance and the analysis is made public and open to third-party review (Marcelo and others 2016). Adequate social and environmental risk management is also critical to managing costs, ensuring popular support, and ensuring the likelihood of a project's success.

Box 3.2 Assessing Needs and Proposing a Pipeline—The Case of Infrastructure Australia

In 2008, in response to inadequate coordination in infrastructure planning, the Australian government created Infrastructure Australia, an independent statutory body, whose role is to provide independent research and advice to all levels of government as well as to investors and owners of infrastructure on the projects and reforms Australia needs to fill the infrastructure gap. Its responsibilities include auditing the country's infrastructure needs and performance and developing a rolling 15-year infrastructure plan that identifies Australia's national and state-level infrastructure priorities in transport, including energy, telecommunications, and water. Implementation of the plan requires that the federal government and/or the subnational governments subsequently make it official policy.

Infrastructure Australia is tasked with identifying Australia's long-term infrastructure needs through an infrastructure audit. This audit is based on an analysis of drivers of infrastructure demand, such as population and economic growth, and looks out to 2031. It has served as a key input to Australia's current Infrastructure Plan, which contains a package of reforms regarding how infrastructure is financed, delivered, and used.

The strategy developed in the plan considers a wide range of options and instruments, including institutional and regulatory reforms, as well as investments. The longer-term view helped move beyond the more common project-centered approach and enabled a more integrated view of how infrastructure across various sectors can contribute to the country's development. Infrastructure Australia then developed an Infrastructure Priority List of initiatives and projects in collaboration with state and territory governments and industry that considers three dimensions: strategic fit; economic, social, and environmental value; and ability to deliver.

The plan identified a number of complex reforms that could deliver significant productivity benefits country wide but which were politically challenging. To overcome this, Infrastructure Australia proposed a three-tiered approach that called on the national government to leverage its investment in infrastructure to encourage state and local governments to implement the reforms identified in the plan. In addition, Infrastructure Australia emphasized the need for early community engagement—which can improve the quality of planning and reduce opposition.

box continues next page

Rethinking Infrastructure in Latin America and the Caribbean
http://dx.doi.org/10.1596/978-1-4648-1101-2

Box 3.2 Assessing Needs and Proposing a Pipeline—The Case of Infrastructure Australia *(continued)*

Key strengths of the Australian system include the following:

- *Insulation from political pressures.* As an independent body, Infrastructure Australia is, in principle, insulated from the political process and can therefore assess infrastructure needs and develop recommendations on the basis of objective criteria.
- *A structured approach.* Infrastructure Australia applied a sequenced and structured approach to infrastructure planning by framing investment choices within a long-term assessment of needs (the Audit) and a considered evaluation of the various options for addressing those needs that is guided by a set of long-term goals (the Plan).
- *An integrated strategy.* By considering all infrastructure sectors within a single plan that is guided by a set of long-term ambitions, the Infrastructure Plan provides for an integrated perspective of infrastructure.

Such a holistic and integrated approach encourages greater alignment across sectors and investments and improves the scope for generating synergies.

Source: OECD 2017.

Conclusions

Good infrastructure is key to Latin America's ambitions in terms of growth, inclusiveness, and environmental sustainability. But money is not necessarily the missing ingredient for the region to achieve its ambitions. More focused goals and efficient strategies can substantially reduce financing needs. In addition, upstream reforms will enable Latin America to both improve spending efficiency and attract private financing on better terms—whether through PPPs or commercial borrowing by public enterprises. And efforts to improve public investment institutions and frameworks—notably budgeting and procurement systems—should enable the region to substantially stretch the resources it already allocates to infrastructure.

This report provides a framework for countries wishing to improve their infrastructure performance despite fiscal constraints. It does so by recommending a careful definition of priorities, highlighting steps that can be taken to improve efficiency, and noting the need to carefully chose between what should be funded by users versus taxpayers. But this report could usefully be complemented by more in-depth, country or regional, analysis of the following issues:

- Quality of service—as chapter 1 makes clear, limited information is available on the quality of service, raising the question of whether infrastructure access levels paint a full picture of how well the region is doing.
- How to manage the region's sprawling urban development—a forthcoming World Bank report on urbanization will shed some light on this evolution based on new data and analysis.

- Subsidies—the limited data available suggest that subsidies, often poorly targeted, remain substantial in a number of countries, and may be larger than what the region invests in infrastructure.
- Public spending efficiency and fiscal space available for capital spending—this report is limited to somewhat anecdotal evidence regarding public spending efficiency, and it falls far short of a full analysis of fiscal space and of countries' ability to rebalance public spending in favor of capital spending.

Public expenditure surveys focused on infrastructure would be extremely valuable tools in helping governments understand where institutional weaknesses lie and the extent to which efficiency gains could help achieve infrastructure goals.

Notes

1. This discussion was developed based on Leigland, Trémolet, and Ikeda (2016).

2. "Commercial" capital or financing is meant here as capital or financing that subjects the borrower (for example, a utility) to the discipline of the market. It includes project and corporate finance, commercial bank financing, project and corporate bond issuance, and private equity; for example, through stock exchange listings or direct investment. It would preclude financing from state-owned commercial banks, national development banks, or sovereign wealth funds investing in domestic jurisdictions (but not abroad) as well as MDB or DFI financing where there is an explicit or inferred sovereign counter guarantee.

3. In addition, there may be potential to capture the value created through infrastructure investments in less traditional ways (land-value capture, congestion charging, parking fees) or through the commercial exploitation of infrastructure assets (advertising, real estate).

4. Data from Andrés, Schwartz, and Guasch (2013) for electricity and IBNET for water. In 2014, the private sector accounted for 65 percent of electricity generation according to industry data.

5. These principles aim to establish a clear, predictable, and legitimate institutional framework; ground the selection of public–private partnerships in "value for money," and minimize fiscal risks. For more details, see http://www.oecd.org/gov /budgeting/oecd-principles-for-public-governance-of-public-private-partnerships .htm.

References

Andrés, Luis, Dan Biller, and Matias Herrera Dappe. 2016. "A Methodological Framework for Prioritizing Infrastructure Investment." *Journal of Infrastructure Development* 8 (2): 111–17.

Andrés, Luis, Jordan Schwartz, and J. Luis Guasch. 2013. *Uncovering the Drivers of Utility Performance: Lessons from Latin America and the Caribbean on the Role of the Private Sector*, Regulation, and Governance in the Power, Water, and Telecommunication Sectors. Washington, DC: World Bank.

Araya, Gonzalo, Jordan Schwartz, and Luis Andrés. 2013. "The Effects of Country Risk and Conflict on Infrastructure PPPs." Policy Research Working Paper 6569, World Bank, Washington, DC.

Broad, Oliver, Gustavo de Moura, and Mark Howells. 2016. "Investment Needs in the Energy Sector along Multiple Socio-economic Pathways." Background paper commissioned for this report, KTH Royal Institute of Technology, Stockholm.

Fay, Marianne, and Stéphane Straub. 2016. "Rising Incomes and the Demand for Infrastructure of Latin American Households." Background paper commissioned for this report, World Bank, Washington, DC.

Garcia-Kilroy, Catiana, and Heinz Rudolph. 2017. *Infrastructure Finance in Latin America and the Caribbean: Challenges and Opportunities*. Washington, DC: World Bank.

Heymans, Chris, Rolfe Eberhard, David Ehrhardt, and Shannon Riley. 2016. *Providing Water to Poor People in African Cities Effectively: Lessons from Utility Reforms*. Washington, DC: World Bank. https://openknowledge.worldbank.org/handle/10986/25115.

Hutton, Guy, and Mili Varughese. 2016. *The Costs of Meeting the 2030 Sustainable Development Goal Targets on Drinking Water, Sanitation, and Hygiene*. Technical Paper, Water and Sanitation Program, World Bank, Washington, DC.

IMF (International Monetary Fund). 2014. *World Economic Outlook: Legacies, Clouds, Uncertainties*. Washington, DC: IMF.

Leigland, James, Sophie Trémolet, and John Ikeda. 2016. "Achieving Universal Access to Water and Sanitation by 2030: The Role of Blended Finance." Discussion Paper, Water Global Practice, World Bank, Washington, DC. http://documents.worldbank.org/curated/en/978521472029369304/pdf/107971-WP-P159188-PUBLIC.pdf.

Marcelo, G. Darwin, Xavier C. Mandri-Perrott, Ruth S. House, and Jordan Z. Schwartz. 2016. "Prioritizing Infrastructure Investment: A Framework for Government Decision Making." Policy Research Working Paper 7674, World Bank, Washington, DC. http://documents.worldbank.org/curated/en/805021467996728921/pdf/WPS7674.pdf.

Marulanda, Catalina, Beatriz Eraso, Emanuela Monteiro, and Pablo Gluzmann. 2015. "LAC Infrastructure Gap: A Territorial Development Perspective." Background paper commissioned for this report, World Bank, Washington, DC.

OECD (Organisation for Economic Co-operation and Development). 2017. "Infrastructure Governance in Chile," OECD, Paris.

World Bank. 2017. "Infrastructure Finance: Guiding Principles for the World Bank Group—A Cascade Decision-Making Approach." World Bank, Washington, DC.

Public Expenditure Reviews Examined for This Report

World Bank. 2015. *Haiti—Towards Greater Fiscal Sustainability and Equity: A Discussion of Public Finance*. Vols. 1 and 2 of *Better Spending, Better Services—A Review of Public Finances in Haiti*. Washington, DC: World Bank. https://hubs.worldbank.org/docs/imagebank/pages/docprofile.aspx?nodeid=24732446.

———. 2015. *El Salvador—Estudio de gasto público social y sus instituciones*. Washington, DC: World Bank. https://hubs.worldbank.org/docs/imagebank/pages/docprofile.aspx?nodeid= 25011533.

———. 2014. *Ceara PforR: Full Fiduciary Systems Assessment*. Washington, DC: World Bank. http://documents.worldbank.org/curated/en/346981468238750993/pdf/892790WP0P12080ry0Assessment0final.pdf.

———. 2014. *Honduras—Central America Social Expenditures and Institutional Review*. Washington, DC: World Bank. https://hubs.worldbank.org/docs/imagebank/pages/docprofile.aspx?nodeid=23839196.

———. 2014. *Brazil's Productivity Challenge: Selected Issues in Understanding and Improving Productivity*. Washington, DC: World Bank. https://hubs.worldbank.org/docs/imagebank/pages/docprofile.aspx?nodeid=19717534.

———. 2013. *Uruguay—Public Expenditure Review: Mitigating Fiscal Risks*. Washington, DC: World Bank. https://hubs.worldbank.org/docs/imagebank/pages/docprofile.aspx?nodeid=17731695.

———. 2013. *Towards Better Expenditure Quality: Guatemala Public Expenditure Review*. Washington, DC: World Bank. https://hubs.worldbank.org/docs/imagebank/pages/docprofile.aspx?nodeid=17817212.

———. 2013. *The Quest for Optimal Tax and Expenditure Policies for Shared Prosperity*. Vol. 1 of *A Public Expenditure Review for Paraguay*. Washington, DC: World Bank. https://hubs.worldbank.org/docs/imagebank/pages/docprofile.aspx?nodeid=18706123.

———. 2013. *Public Expenditures for Decentralized Governance in Honduras: Towards Restoring Fiscal Consolidation*. Washington, DC: World Bank. http://documents.worldbank.org/curated/en/794291468037567297/pdf/826620REVISED00PER0HN0english0FINAL.pdf.

————. 2013. *Nicaragua—Agriculture Public Expenditure Review*. Washington, DC: World Bank. https://hubs.worldbank.org/docs/imagebank/pages/docprofile.aspx ?nodeid23927226.

————. 2013. *Belize—PPIAF SNTA Municipal Finance: Report of RESP Activity*. Washington, DC: World Bank. https://hubs.worldbank.org/docs/imagebank/pages /docprofile.aspx?nodeid=17723213.

————. 2013. *Agricultural Productivity and Family Farms in Brazil: Creating Opportunities and Closing Gaps*. Washington, DC: World Bank. https://hubs.worldbank.org/docs /imagebank/pages/docprofile.aspx?nodeid=17852509.

————. 2012. *Peru—Public Expenditure Review for Peru: Spending for Results*. Washington, DC: World Bank. https://hubs.worldbank.org/docs/imagebank/pages /docprofile.aspx?nodeid=17204328.

————. 2012. *Mexico—Social Protection System in Health and the Transformation of State Health Systems*. Washington, DC: World Bank. https://hubs.worldbank.org/docs /imagebank/pages/docprofile.aspx?nodeid=17591008.

————. 2012. *Guatemala—Public Expenditure Review*. Washington, DC: World Bank. https://hubs.worldbank.org/docs/imagebank/pages/docprofile.aspx?nodeid=16593124.

————. 2010. *Peru—The Decentralization Process and Its Links with Public Expenditure Efficiency*. Washington, DC: World Bank. https://hubs.worldbank.org/docs/imagebank /pages/docprofile.aspx?nodeid=16373412.

————. 2010. *Peru—Evaluación del Presupuesto Participativo y su relación con el presupuesto por resultados*. Washington, DC: World Bank. https://hubs.worldbank.org/docs /imagebank/pages/docprofile.aspx?nodeid=12996952.

————. 2010. *Nicaragua—Selected Issues in Social Sectors Management: Programmatic Social NLTA Implementation Report*. Washington, DC: World Bank. https://hubs .worldbank.org/docs/imagebank/pages/docprofile.aspx?nodeid=16579617.

————. 2010. *Main Report*. Vol. 1 of *Public Expenditure Tracking and Service Delivery Survey: Education and Health in Honduras*. Washington, DC: World Bank. https:// hubs.worldbank.org/docs/imagebank/pages/docprofile.aspx?nodeid=15165197.

————. 2010. *Main Report*. Vol. 1 of *El Salvador—Enhancing the Efficiency and Targeting of Expenditures: Public Expenditure Review*. Washington, DC: World Bank. https://hubs .worldbank.org/docs/imagebank/pages/docprofile.aspx?nodeid=16242844.

————. 2009. *Mexico—Agriculture and Rural Development Public Expenditure Review*. Washington, DC: World Bank. https://hubs.worldbank.org/docs/imagebank/pages /docprofile.aspx?nodeid=11616349.

————. 2008. *Nicaragua—Social Protection Public Expenditure Review*. Washington, DC: World Bank. https://hubs.worldbank.org/docs/imagebank/pages/docprofile.aspx ?nodeid=16579503.

————. 2008. *Nicaragua—Public Expenditure Review 2001–2006*. Washington, DC: World Bank. https://hubs.worldbank.org/docs/imagebank/pages/docprofile.aspx ?nodeid=9701111.

————. 2008. *Nicaragua—Análisis del Gasto Público Social*. Washington, DC: World Bank. https://hubs.worldbank.org/docs/imagebank/pages/docprofile.aspx?nodeid =16588702.

————. 2008. *Main Report*. Vol. 1 of *Brazil—Toward a More Inclusive and Effective Participatory Budget in Porto Alegre*. Washington, DC: World Bank. https://hubs .worldbank.org/docs/imagebank/pages/docprofile.aspx?nodeid=9053955.

———. 2008. *Costa Rica—Public Expenditure Review: Enhancing the Efficiency of Expenditures.* Washington, DC: World Bank. https://hubs.worldbank.org/docs/imagebank/pages/docprofile.aspx?nodeid=9543594.

———. 2007. *Honduras: Public Expenditure Review Executive Summary and Main Report.* Washington, DC: World Bank. https://hubs.worldbank.org/docs/imagebank/pages/docprofile.aspx?nodeid=8961697.

———. 2006. *Paraguay—Public Expenditure Review: Main Report.* Washington, DC: World Bank. https://hubs.worldbank.org/docs/imagebank/pages/docprofile.aspx?nodeid=6884196.

———. 2006. *Mexico—Water Public Expenditure Review.* Washington, DC: World Bank. https://hubs.worldbank.org/docs/imagebank/pages/docprofile.aspx?nodeid=17234229.

Procurement Performance of Latin American Countries: Relatively Good, but with Wide Variation across Countries and Indicators

Although reforms have been undertaken by a number of countries throughout Latin America, several areas can be further improved. The World Bank's *Benchmarking Public Procurement 2017* found that suppliers identify obstacles such as excessive bureaucracy and red tape in Colombia and Honduras; payment delays in Argentina, the Dominican Republic, and Jamaica; lack of transparency and opaque tendering processes in Brazil and Mexico; lack of efficiency in Barbados and Puerto Rico; and the list goes on.

More generally, the *Benchmarking Public Procurement 2017* data (see box B.1) reveal that many Latin American countries still face challenges in establishing legal and regulatory environments that enhance efficient and transparent public procurement markets. On average, however, the region compares reasonably well with other regions in all but one area measured: the region's score is less than half that of Organisation for Economic Co-operation and Development (OECD) countries for recurrent delays in payments (figure B.1). Timely payment of suppliers encourages firms' participation in tenders, which in turn will lead to more competition and better value for money for the purchasing entity (Connell 2014). Payments take place within the recognized good practice time frame of 30 days in only five economies in the region (Belize, Grenada, Nicaragua, Peru, and the Bahamas) and can take six months or longer in the region's worse performers (the Dominican Republic and Trinidad and Tobago).

In addition, the region could improve its performance with respect to online access to information and services. Digital tools can streamline public spending, make it more transparent and evidence based, and integrate it with information on market conditions. Only 13 out of 30 Latin American and Caribbean

Box B.1 What Is the Benchmarking Public Procurement Database?

The *Benchmarking Public Procurement* 2017 (BPP)[a] initiative is a global assessment of public procurement regulatory frameworks across 180 economies—of which 30 are in Latin America. It focuses on six key areas of the public procurement process for a tender of works, including the following:

- *Needs assessment, call for tender, and bid preparation* indicators assess the quality, adequacy, and transparency of the information provided by the procuring entity to prospective bidders.
- *Bid submission* indicators examine the requirements that suppliers must meet in order to bid effectively and avoid having their bid rejected.
- *Bid opening, evaluation, and contract award* indicators measure the extent to which the regulatory framework and procedures provide a fair and transparent bid opening and evaluation process, as well as whether once the best has been identified, the contract is awarded transparently and the losing bidders are informed of the procuring entity's decision.
- *Content and management of the procurement* contract indicators focus on several aspects during the contract execution phase related to the modification and termination of the procurement contract and the procedure for accepting the completion of works.
- *Performance guarantee* indicators examine the existence and requirements of the performance guarantee.
- *Payment of suppliers* indicators focus on the time and procedure needed for suppliers to receive payment during the contract execution phase.

a. *Benchmarking Public Procurement* initiative is housed in the World Bank Group's (WBG) Development Economics Global Indicators department (DECIG). It was developed at the request of the G20 Anti-Corruption Working Group and builds on the WBG's Doing Business flagship methodology. For more information about the initiative, please visit http://bpp.worldbank.org.

countries evaluated make all procurement information available online, and 7 have yet to establish an electronic portal dedicated to public procurement. The same goes for online services during the bid submission, bid evaluation, and award and contract management phases. Just as suppliers need to access information online, they should be able to conduct the procurement process online, regardless of what is being procured by the government.

The availability of electronic tendering is not as widespread for the procurement of works as it is for the procurement of goods. In Chile for example, the electronic submission of bids has become the rule for the procurement of goods but not for the procurement of works. Similarly, when it comes to the bid opening session, bids are sometimes opened electronically in Brazil, Costa Rica, Ecuador, Jamaica, Mexico, and Uruguay and never in the remaining 24 economies.

Performance guarantees, which are particularly important for public works, is another area where the benchmarking data highlight great variation among

Figure B.1 Latin America's Regional Performance Is on Par with Others, Except When It Comes to Timely Payment of Suppliers

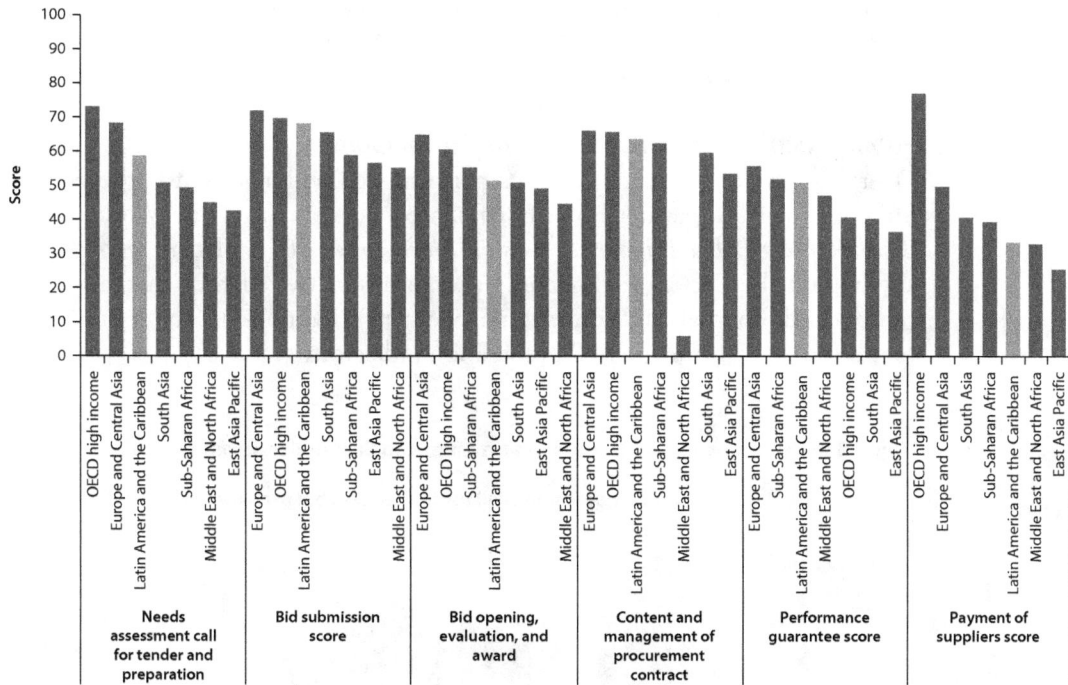

Source: World bank 2017a.
Note: For each indicator developed, the scores of individual questions are averaged and multiplied by 100, resulting in a final score ranging from 0 to 100. The economies at the top of the range (with scores approaching 100) are considered to have a regulatory framework that closely aligns with internationally recognized good practices, whereas the economies at the bottom of the range (scores closer to 0) have significant room for improvement in the particular area measured. OECD = Organisation for Economic Co-operation and Development.

the different players in the region (figure B.2). Performance guarantees during the contract execution phase are an important tool to ensure delivery of service per contract terms and protect parties in case of delays in execution. All 30 economies measured in Latin America by the *Benchmarking Public Procurement* initiative impose a performance guarantee requirement during the contract execution phase. Performance guarantees should be well regulated in order to protect suppliers and avoid creating an additional impediment for them. For example, it is important for suppliers to have a choice with regard to the form of performance guarantees. Costa Rica and Ecuador are the economies that provide the most options for the form of the guarantee, which can include a certified check, a certificate of deposit, or a letter of credit, among others. It is also critical that the legal framework set a timeframe for the purchasing entity to return the performance guarantee after the execution of the contract. Only 11 countries, such as El Salvador, Mexico, and Panama, impose such a time limit.

Rethinking Infrastructure in Latin America and the Caribbean
http://dx.doi.org/10.1596/978-1-4648-1101-2

Regional averages hide the wide disparity between countries in the region. Out of the 30 economies measured, Ecuador, for example, shows high scores in most areas measured. Similarly, Costa Rica appears in the top five performing economies across three areas. Antigua and Barbuda and St. Lucia, on the other hand, show the weakest performance.

Public Procurement of Public-Private Partnerships

Overall, economies in Latin America perform well with respect to procurement for public-private partnerships (PPPs) based on data from the World Bank's *Benchmarking Public-Private Partnership Procurement 2017*, placing second globally behind the OECD high-income economies in two of four thematic areas (unsolicited proposals and contract management) (figure B.3).[1] The region's lowest performance is for the PPP preparation indicators.

Figure B.2 Variations Appear between Latin American Economies across Thematic Areas

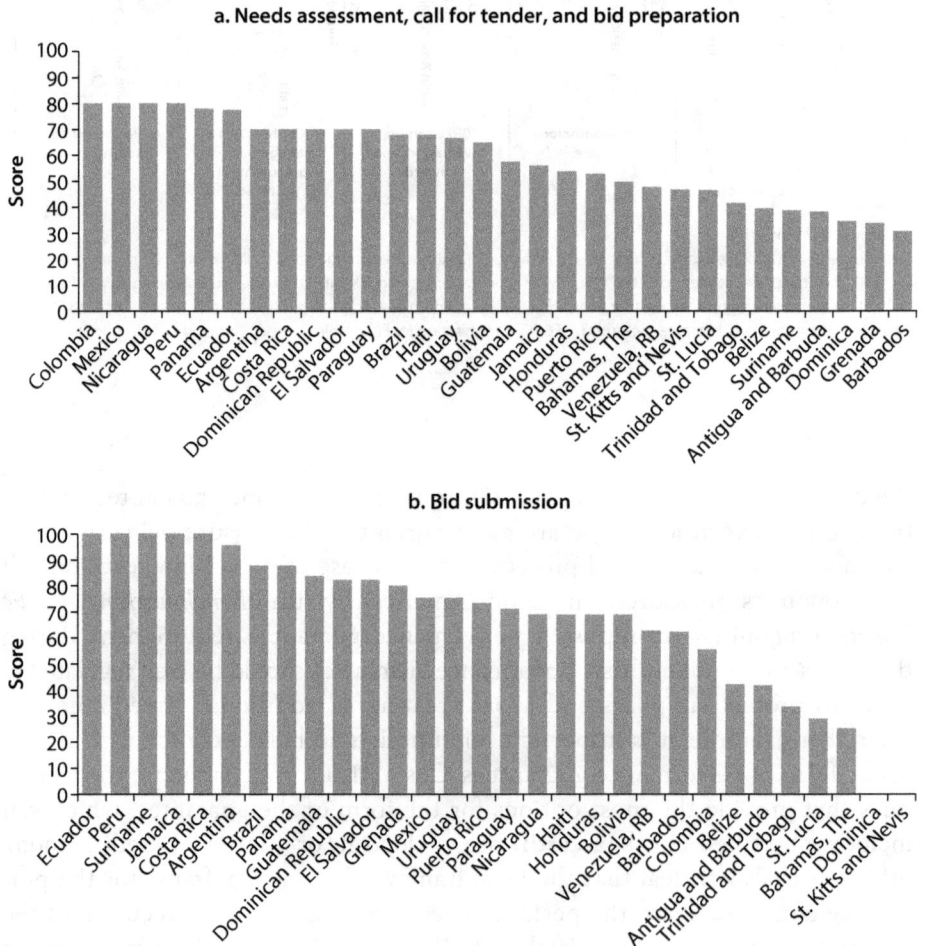

a. Needs assessment, call for tender, and bid preparation

b. Bid submission

figure continues next page

Figure B.2 Variations Appear between Latin American Economies across Thematic Areas *(continued)*

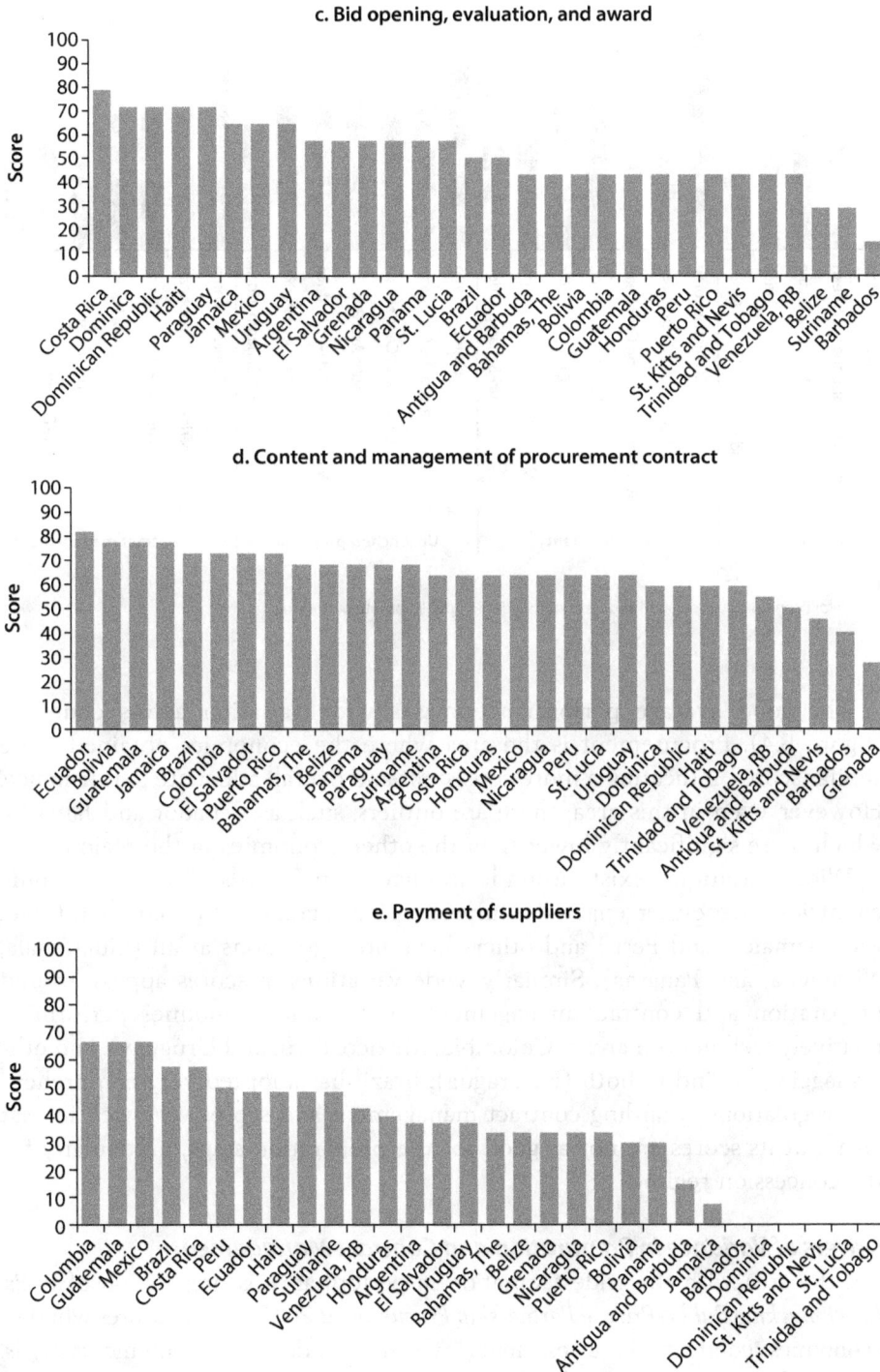

c. Bid opening, evaluation, and award

d. Content and management of procurement contract

e. Payment of suppliers

Source: World Bank 2017b.

Figure B.3 Benchmarking PPP Procurement Scores Vary by Region and Thematic Areas

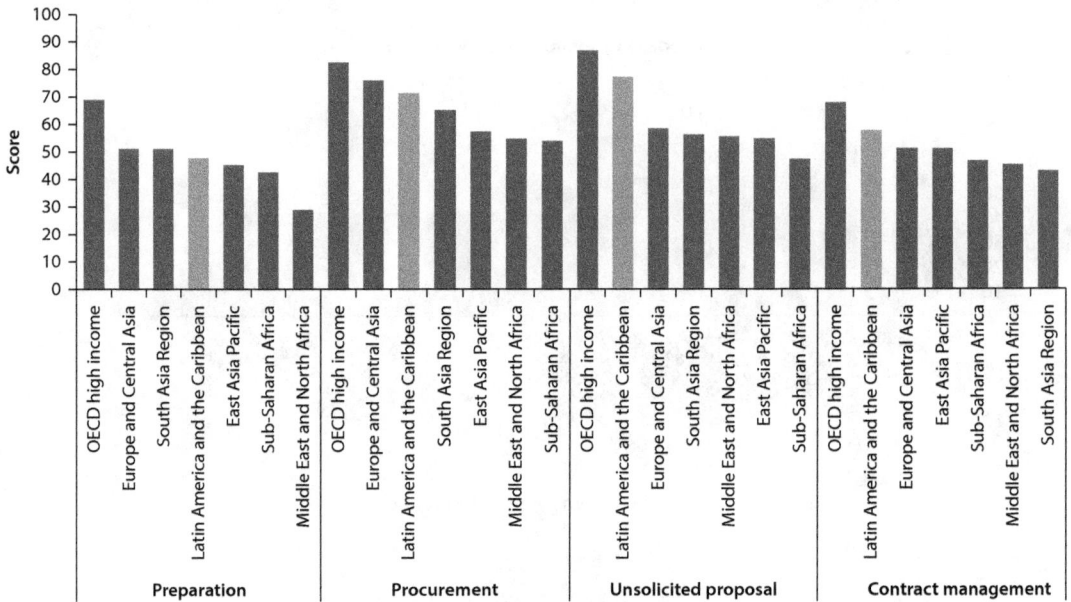

Source: World Bank 2017a.
Note: OECD = Organisation for Economic Co-operation and Development; PPP = public-private partnership.

The good average performance masks wide variation across countries (figure B.4). Procurement is the area where the economies obtained more similar scores, indicating a more consistent and overall adequate performance. However, even in this area, there are outliers, such as Ecuador and Jamaica, which score significantly lower than the other economies in the region.

Wide variations exist around unsolicited proposals, for which some countries have either enacted comprehensive regulations (Colombia, Costa Rica, Jamaica, and Peru) and others have no regulations at all (Guatemala, Nicaragua, and Panama). Similarly, wide variations in scores appear around preparation and contract management, with some economies performing relatively well in both areas (Colombia, Mexico, Peru, and Uruguay), and others lagging behind in both (Nicaragua). Brazil has adopted very comprehensive regulations regarding contract management and scores very well in that area, but its scores are not as good for the preparation stage, particularly for the concession regime.

Drivers of Variance in Preparation and Contract Management

But the area with the widest variation in performance is preparation of PPPs. *Benchmarking Public-Private Partnership Procurement 2017* data measures whether economies conduct six assessments, which include socioeconomic analysis, affordability assessment, risk identification, financial viability or bankability assessment, comparative assessment, and market assessment. Some economies

Figure B.4 Variation also Emerges across the Region by Thematic Area

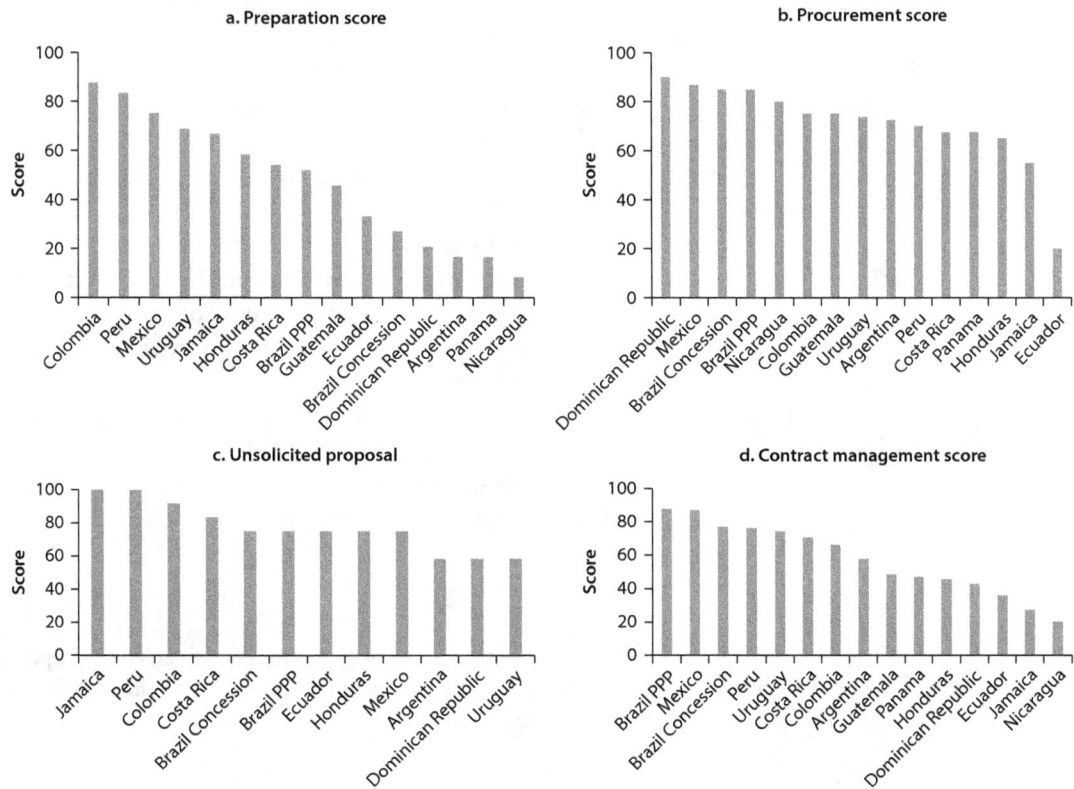

a. Preparation score

b. Procurement score

c. Unsolicited proposal

d. Contract management score

Source: World Bank 2017a.

Note: The following economies do not have a regulatory framework that explicitly mentions unsolicited proposals (unsolicited proposals are not regulated and therefore not scored in Guatemala, Nicaragua, Panama).

conduct almost all of these assessments (such as Mexico and Jamaica), while others conduct only one of them (Panama and Nicaragua), or none at all (the Dominican Republic). And in Nicaragua, for example, the government is not required to integrate the prioritization of PPP projects with other public investment projects, nor are the assessments required.

Our analysis also examines whether the Ministry of Finance, or a central budgetary authority, needs to approve the PPP project before a procurement process is launched. According to our assessment, such an approval is not required in 4 of the 14 economies measured (Argentina, the Dominican Republic, Ecuador, and Nicaragua).

Contract management is another area where a significant difference in performance exists amongst economies. Although there are several factors that lead to the lower performance of some economies in this area, a few particular ones stand out. Honduras and Jamaica are the economies where the regulatory framework does not expressly establish grounds for the termination of a PPP contract. Our data also measure whether the regulatory framework establishes a specific dispute resolution mechanism, and we find that Colombia, Jamaica, Nicaragua, and Panama do not have such a system. Lastly, our data examine whether the regulatory framework expressly regulates the modification or renegotiation of a PPP contract, as well as the three circumstances that could be regulated (a change in the scope/object of contract, a change in the risk allocation of the contract, a change in the investment plan or duration of the contract). The regulatory frameworks in Ecuador, Guatemala, Honduras, and Nicaragua do not regulate the modification/renegotiation of a PPP contract.

Overall, the regulatory frameworks governing the procurement of PPPs in Latin America are better than in other regions of the globe. However, there is room for improvement in all areas, to increase the quality of the regulatory framework to match those that exist in the OECD high-income economies. Preparation of PPPs appears to be the area where the region as a whole could focus its efforts in order to improve regulatory frameworks for PPPs. While the regulatory frameworks for PPPs in economies like Colombia, Mexico, Uruguay, and Peru are comparable to that of more mature markets, some other economies clearly lag behind in several aspects (Jamaica and Nicaragua).

Note

1. The Benchmarking PPP procurement data assess governments' capacity to prepare, procure, and manage PPP projects. http://bpp.worldbank.org/~/media/WBG/BPP /Documents/Reports/BenchmarkingPPP2017.pdf.

References

Connell, William. 2014. "European Economy: The Economic Impact of Late Payments." Economic Paper 531, European Commission, Brussels.

World Bank. 2017a. *Benchmarking Public-Private Partnerships Procurement*. World Bank, Washington, D.C. http://bpp.financeandprivatesector.org/~/media/WBG /BPP/Documents/Reports/BenchmarkingPPP2017Fullreport.pdf?la=en.

———. 2017b. *Benchmarking Public Procurement 2017*. World Bank, Washington, D.C. http://bpp.financeandprivatesector.org/~/media/WBG/BPP/Documents/Reports/Ben chmarking-Public-Procurement-2017.pdf.

Environmental Benefits Statement

The World Bank Group is committed to reducing its environmental footprint. In support of this commitment, we leverage electronic publishing options and print-on-demand technology, which is located in regional hubs worldwide. Together, these initiatives enable print runs to be lowered and shipping distances decreased, resulting in reduced paper consumption, chemical use, greenhouse gas emissions, and waste.

We follow the recommended standards for paper use set by the Green Press Initiative. The majority of our books are printed on Forest Stewardship Council (FSC)–certified paper, with nearly all containing 50–100 percent recycled content. The recycled fiber in our book paper is either unbleached or bleached using totally chlorine-free (TCF), processed chlorine–free (PCF), or enhanced elemental chlorine–free (EECF) processes.

More information about the Bank's environmental philosophy can be found at http://www.worldbank.org/corporateresponsibility.

green
press
INITIATIVE